we love you!

M. B.   11/21/21

PROVERBS
of
SUCCESS

Proverbs of Success is published under Aspire, a sectionalized division under Di Angelo Publications, Inc.

Aspire is an imprint of Di Angelo Publications.
Copyright @ 2021.
All rights reserved.
Printed in United States of America.

Di Angelo Publications
4265 San Felipe #1100
Houston, TX 77027

Library of Congress
Proverbs of Success
Hardback - First Edition
ISBN: 978-1-942549-95-6

Words: Mike Ogbebor
Cover Design: Savina Deinova
Interior Design: Kimberly James
Developmental Editor: Ashley Crantas
Editors: Stephanie Yoxen

Downloadable via Kindle, NOOK and Google Play.

No part of this publication may be reproduced, distributed or transmitted in any form or by any means without the prior written consent of the publisher, except in the case of brief quotations embodied in critical reviews and certain other noncommercial uses permitted by copyright law. For permissions requests, contact info@diangelopublications.com.

For educational, business, and bulk orders, contact sales@diangelopublications.com.

1. Self Help --- Personal Growth --- Success
2. Self Help --- Self Management --- General
3. Body, Mind & Spirit --- Inspiration & Personal Growth
4,. Biography & Autobiography --- African American & Black

United States of America with int. distribution.

PROVERBS

of

SUCCESS

MIKE OGBEBOR

Acknowledgments

This book is dedicated to the love of my life, Galia, and our three extraordinary kids: Mike Jr., Israel, and Michelle. You guys are my foundation and Why.

My father and mother, Joe and Eunice Ogbebor: Thank you for showing me at an early age what success looks like.

Special thanks to Dr. Christian and Dr. Itohan Ogbebor, Godwin Ogbebor, Dr. Joseph and Dr. Joyce Voukep, Dr. Walter and Luda Afedo, Robert and Aksana Mensah, and Diana Afedo.

THE JOURNEY OF A THOUSAND MILES STARTS WITH ONE ACTION

#GOBEYONDYESTERDAY

Contents

	Foreword	11
	My Story	13
1.	Action and Words	19
2.	Mindset	33
3.	Belief System	53
4.	Partnerships & Associations	71
5.	Determination	87
6.	The Mirage of Perfection	105
7.	Mistakes and Failures	119
8.	Timing	131
9.	Closed Doors	139
10.	Mentors	153
11.	Faith	165
	Closing Remarks	181
	References	183

Foreword

Count this book out of the typical *"Seven Steps to Making It in Life"* books you can find on the internet these days. This book is not a shortcut to anything. It covers all you need to know about success. It is a collection of principles, facts, and ideas that govern attaining and maintaining success.

Throughout this book, you will find references to the Book of Proverbs, as well as numerous other Biblical books. Proverbs has evidence that God is not anti-success, especially anti-financial success, like some people may think. Yes, God wants us to be humble, but He is also the strong foundation upon which every success should be built.

If you are reading *Proverbs of Success,* you are one of the few looking to become the most successful version of yourself. Whatever the motive, it is safe to say you are in luck. Yes, you read that correctly. If there is anything you should look forward to after reading this book, it is how profoundly your perception of success will change. This book will shape your ideas and change your view of success.

My candid advice for you: be willing to let go of all that you have learned about success thus far. Prepare your mind for a reset; you will gain much more when you read with an open mind.

The idea of success has, over time, been bastardized and made subject to false beliefs. To some, success is a reward. To others, it is something to seize at all costs, no matter the process—this is exactly why we see people end up in all kinds of vices and shameful acts.

Success is not only about making money. You will become covetous if you think of success this way. A successful person is one who fulfills his own unique purpose and achieves his dream in life. Am I saying you should remain poor while fulfilling your purpose? No! All I am saying is: don't reach for the top just because of wealth. Fulfill purpose and passion, and then monetary gain will flow in ceaselessly.

That said, grab a tea, coffee, or FIJI Water, relax in your favorite chair, and see how your life can change with the *Proverbs of Success*.

- David Imonitie

My Story

When I was eleven years old, my father brought my siblings and me from Nigeria to the United States. It was nothing short of a miracle. My father had been well established in Nigeria as a FOREX Bank manager, and my mother was a professor. After praying and hearing from God, they decided to migrate to the United States and start over from nothing, all for the sake of our future. This was a leap of faith, and it changed the trajectory of my entire life. There were two motivations for my parents to migrate to the United States. The first was that my father's place of employment had decided to eliminate the FOREX position he'd had for years. Second, my younger brother had passed away at only two years old while under the supervision of my father's relatives; this was the tipping point that spurred our decision to relocate in search of a new beginning, both financially and emotionally.

The first two years in Houston were arduous. I shared a single room with my four siblings. My mother sold newspapers on the street while attending nursing school. My father worked multiple jobs to make ends meet. As my siblings and I watched my parents go through this, witnessing their constant drive, their discipline, their focus, their steadfast beliefs, and their communication throughout was inspiring. They were relentless and faithful at even the smallest of tasks as if they knew we were watching. They were showing us the blueprint to success.

I learned what hard work and trusting God were all about at a young age.

Then, in the mid-'90s, my mother and father decided to make a change. I remember them applying for a fifty-thousand-dollar bank loan to start their first business, but all banks turned them down. Later that year, a white man from Dallas dressed like a cowboy offered them the loan. At the time, this was unheard of, a white male giving that amount to foreigners with no collateral ties. It was nothing short of a miracle.

The business, our first healthcare and physical medicine clinic, was a huge success. This was the start of a new chapter, and my parents showed us what it looked like to build a foundation of success from scratch; this is how my parents first inspired *Proverbs of Success*.

In late 2006, I was in my second year of medical school. It

was during that time that God impressed on my heart that I should leave school and go back home to assist with the family businesses. I came home, and little did I know that my father would pass away ten months later. This was one of my lowest points and a devastating blow to the family.

But, if we look to God in our lowest moments, He will bring us supernatural peace and comfort in places we do not expect. That same year my father passed, I met my beautiful wife, Galia. We also opened our first dialysis clinic, the inspiration having come from my mother's successful kidney transplant after being on dialysis for over two years! One of my mother's favorite Bible Scriptures is Romans 8:28: "All things work together for good. What the enemy means for evil, God uses for our good."

Shortly after that, God graced us with the opportunity to open our second dialysis clinic in Houston, Texas; a year later we opened the largest dialysis clinic in Africa, which included a nonprofit section to provide the same standard of treatment as our US clinics had to those who could not afford the medical costs.

I believe success is a journey, not a destination. There are several types of success: financial, spiritual, emotional, and physical. I believe we are all created to experience all that success has to offer. This is the reason I have written this book: so that I may share my experiences and principles of success and help others enjoy the journey!

My prayer before we begin: May God bless you and open your mind to understanding and experiencing all levels of success. May this be a road map and a blueprint for you to maximize your success!

I BELIEVE SUCCESS IS A JOURNEY, NOT A DESTINATION. WE ARE ALL CREATED TO EXPERIENCE ALL THAT SUCCESS HAS TO OFFER.

Chapter One
ACTIONS & WORDS

All hard work brings a profit, but mere talk leads only to poverty.
—Book of Proverbs

What better way to start than to talk about the most important part of achieving success? Aligning your actions with your words.

We are all born with the DNA of success, but it is up to each one of us to activate, cultivate, and affirm it every day. I often refer to the DNA of success as "the on switch." This DNA, this switch, has the ability to change your mindset so fundamentally that you will see everything around you with a new perspective. Reflect if anyone or anything has ever changed you in such a way. If not, allow me to be the one to activate it. Repeat this out loud: "I am so happy and grateful right now that I am successful financially, spiritually, emotionally, and physically." Stop whatever it is you are doing right now, *focus*, and repeat this five more times. Let this become your daily affirmation. Consider just how different your everyday life can be if you see the world with the lens of positivity and possibility.

Being able to articulate your desires is the first step in a lifelong journey. In doing so, you attune your mind to your own motivations, and reinforce your daily purpose. But a first step means there are several stages after to conquer. We can't stop at internal metamorphosis. People do not really care what you have to say; they are more concerned with what you do.

Ultimately, your daily actions determine whether your goals will be achieved or if they will remain in the realm of imagination. It is up to you to make sure your everyday actions are in line with your aspirations. When you reflect back on your life, what are you committing yourself to? What takes up your time, attention, and thoughts? Being able to self-assess in this manner will help you make slight, steady adjustments to your habits until your ordinary day is leading you to the path of personal glory.

Rather than going all around telling friends and foes all that you have planned to do, let your actions do the talking. Do not preface it; be about it. Your actions are what people will remember you by, not your words. Now, they might recall you had clever humor or how you sounded like some intellectual philosopher. But if you do not practice what you preach, how much will people believe you?

Recently, I find that people believe affirmations and manifesting are all there is to it. But I'm afraid that's delusion. Both can be powerful, and I appreciate how they reinforce positivity, but these are not the same as putting in the effort. Manifesting, and affirmations in particular, can be mental and emotional progress, but they're a far cry from tangible results.

Imagine a man who dreams of wealth but walks daily towards certain financial disaster. The man wishes for happiness but commits acts that cause him despair. This is far more common than you may think; we are our own greatest enemy. The separation between what we say and think and what we choose can be immense, and this cognitive dissonance can create great unbalance in life. But it can be resolved by altering your attitudes, mentality, and behaviors, as well as taking the time to educate yourself. Preparation through planning and studying will help you set up your mind and schedule so that you can take the proper first steps and adhere to your path.

Get It Done Anyway

If you only have twenty-four hours in a day, your success depends on how you use that twenty-four. You have probably heard people praise Oprah Winfrey, Ted Turner, and Warren Buffet for their achievements, but remember, their days are just as long as yours! The difference between Oprah and the underachieving person is that Oprah uses her twenty-four hours wisely.

Often, grand achievements seem unattainable because they seem so complex, so beyond our capabilities. We don't even know where to start. The key to making an overwhelming project feel realistic is to break it down. To keep focused, you need to have a short list of quantifiable goals. When you try to tackle everything at once, you inevitably flounder. Breaking up your goals, or "chunking" as some folks call it, makes it vastly easier to navigate problems. Hurdles and missteps will no doubt arise, but on a small scale, you can fix them swiftly, prepare for any similar issues, and carry on. Progress is made in little steps and small decisions, not just in leaps and bounds.

The fact is, no one else is going to get you started. Even if you have friends and folks and colleagues who give you all the right information and tell you all the inspiring things you wish to hear, no one will step into your shoes to do what you ought to do for yourself. No one will force you to read the books. No one will drag your feet to start the journey. You just must get it done, anyway.

The Enemy Is Called Procrastination

When you start on a path—whether it is to learn a subject, create a business, or get in shape—the initial headway will thrill you. On the first day, you are as busy as a squirrel bustling from branch to branch. You're thinking, *"Yeah, I'm going to do this. I'm going to kick-start myself right here."* But a week goes by, and you get burned out, and you begin to think, *"Man, this is a little tough."* You take another step, and it feels as though you never had true desire in the first place. The whole process starts to seem beyond your grasp, and you just want to throw in the towel. You wonder what happened to the enthusiasm from the beginning; it has all faded out.

Beloved, there is no substitute for hard work. You show up, you clock in, you get done, and that is all. Anything else is an excuse.

Motivation is a very fickle thing, and you cannot rely on it exclusively. Those who have made it big in today's world understand this, and that is why they keep achieving great feats. Everything goes smoothly when you're excited to put in the effort and make gains. But you need to learn how to function every single day with or without that motivation. Discipline will train your mind to create positive habits until getting up and getting to work is ingrained. With time, it will become instinctual to get up and ensure the daily essentials of building your future are complete.

The truth is, everyone is lazy by default. It is the easiest thing to do—an object at rest stays at rest. But you can't just wait until you feel up to it. The days when you have zero enthusiasm are the days it's most important to stick to the path and stay on track. You will have a great sense of accomplishment and pride for taking those steps when you wanted to avoid responsibility. This self-control will be a factor in so many areas of your life.

We have all got to leave our comfort zones and do what is necessary. My father used to say, "Time waits for no man," and it is not going to wait for you. It is easy to say you will do this the next day or take on that the following week, but guess what: Tomorrow never comes. It becomes today. If you do not act now, you may never do it again. The cure for procrastination is action—you can only defeat the enemy by acting, despite every feeling of fear, resistance, or negativity.

Take a pause right now and think about those we all admire in the world today. They are people who broke the system: people who practiced singing since they were five, people who shot hundreds of basketballs every morning, and people who invented things no one else could have even imagined. All those people had reasons to procrastinate, and should they have given in, no one would talk about them today.

I believe we are all born with goodness inside us, with hidden potentials that can completely change the universe. But life is difficult, and we're thrown curveballs just when we think we have it all figured out. The drive of existing is what fuels our daily ambitions, and if you have been given a dream, do not discount that—you have a dream because you know you can be more. Develop yourself, guard yourself, and teach yourself the skills you need to actualize your dreams. Above all else, do not remain static; gift yourself the capability to be more.

Discipline

Immediate actions crumble procrastination, but they require discipline. Discipline will help you complete tasks well before they're due and prevent you from stalling unnecessarily.

Discipline is the bridge between ideas and accomplishments, and the space that sets intentions and productivity apart. Remember, most good things are upstream. The idle passage of time takes us drifting, but aimless drifting brings us discontentment, jealousy, and disappointment.

The danger lies in looking at an undisciplined day and concluding that no great harm has been done. It does not seem consequential right then, but add up the days to make a year, and add up those years to make a lifetime; perhaps you can now see how repeating today's small failures can easily turn your life into a major disaster.

Success, on the other hand, is just the same process in reverse. By succeeding at your daily goals, you can see what a massive difference it could make in a year.

The first key to discipline is recognizing that you need it—accepting that you're letting things slip, that you're not developing and progressing in the way you want. Whether it is with your career, life skills, financial literacy, relationships, or hobbies, you may not even realize your goals have been in decline because descent is so often stagnation. Months or years can go by before you look up and realize you haven't moved at all.

The second key is the commitment to master the circumstances of your daily life. You need to make a stand against your own shortcomings, your own doubt and apathy. You need to recognize and harness the opportunities. Believe that you can make something of the sun and the rain—the good, as well as what comes in the guise of misfortune.

Discipline affects many things, but the most pivotal of them all is your mindset. Discipline is a building block for self-confidence. The authentic pride that you'll feel for staying the course and executing your plans is nearly as rewarding as accomplishing your objectives.

Discipline alters your life path. It won't be an easy win, and you won't automatically get to your destination, but you'll discover that you can control the direction of your life. It teaches you that you can make meaningful, long-lasting changes as long as you take your time and stay focused. If you are the type that goes anywhere that happens to suit your comfort, you may end up wondering why your life seems to lack stability. Discipline helps you determine your personal course and will give you the awareness and bravery to take that sharp turn when you are close to missing an opportunity.

We can learn a lot about discipline and inner motivation from nature. Every living thing is striving. A tree grows as large as it can; an eagle flies as high as it is able. Everything endeavors to become all it can be, and that constant striving is what discipline is all about. We are training ourselves to fulfill our natural potential and become our best possible selves.

Discipline opens doors you may normally disregard and taps into the unlimited power of commitment. The human will in action—driven by inspiration, tempered by reason, enticed by desire, and guided by intelligence—can bring you to that high and lofty place called "the good life." Discipline is both the instigation and the continuing process that brings all good things. While starting may sometimes feel like a walk in the park, continuing on is not child's play. We all have what it takes to get started. Be not *"If I could, I would; if I would, I could"*—but rather, *"If I will, I can."* So, start the process, and do not let yourself stray. Be intelligent, adapt to new challenges, but don't let yourself quit when it gets hard.

Developing Self-Confidence

Confidence is not walking into a room thinking you are better than anyone; it is walking in knowing that you do not have to compare yourself to anyone. Measuring yourself by other's standards and achievements will deteriorate your self-worth. So often young people who are striving to improve become awash with envy, doubt, and bitterness because they are always comparing their achievements to that of their peers. This is not the path to betterment. The Bible says in 2 Corinthians 10:12 that those who compare themselves with themselves are not wise, and that's the bitter truth.

Confidence is having no thought of comparison or competition whatsoever—you are not above anyone, you are not below anyone, you are just a king in your own space. When you can get to the place in your life where you no longer have any desire to compare yourself to others, where you are good enough not to others, but to yourself, you will be able to make decisions purely for your best interests. Comparisons will only make you see the bad in yourself—your flaws and insecurities. And no matter how much effort you have put into getting better, you will still find reasons to undersell your successes if you keep comparing. Continuing to stack up your progress against others' will make you constantly depressed over everyone else's achievements, and rather than being inspired and finding the strength to succeed, you will be discouraged.

When it comes to boosting self-confidence and changing your world, your words matter; words are like seeds, and the more time you spend mulling them over and believing in them, the faster they'll take root. When you speak, you make your mind conscious of the matter, and that is eventually going to become your reality. Whether you realize it or not, you prophesy your future by the words you speak.

It is a benefit to say things like, *"I'm blessed," "I'm strong," "I will accomplish my dreams," "I'm getting out of debt,"* and so on. It is much more than being positive; your life will move in the direction of your words.

Sadly, too many people go around these days prophesying just the opposite—*"I can't catch a break," "I will never get back in shape," "Business is slow," "I'll probably get laid off…"* You must be familiar with the words "Never say never." As ordinary as it seems, that five-letter word has done more harm than good to far too many fortunes. People speak carelessly about what they are not yet able to achieve and what they find difficult to accomplish, failing to recognize that the words they speak will only make things worse. How do you find a solution when you are focused on the problem? How do you make headway when your words are nothing but bitter remarks? You cannot talk defeat and expect to have victory. Words are powerful instruments in the mouth of every man, and they should be treated as such.

We all have this negative self-talk that goes on in our heads. And sometimes we are forced to doubt even the things we once boasted about. But enough people tell us about our inabilities; we do not have to tell ourselves, too. If you are passionate about success and wish to have that level of confidence that allows you to act in the middle of uncertainties, you must learn to speak positively. Positive talk is not merely about muttering words. During most motivational speeches, you are asked to recite after the speaker and manifest all that they know to be possible, but if you do not believe in it, saying it will be a sheer waste of time. Words flow from a source, and that is the heart. The master of my fate is my own conviction. If I do not believe it, no one else will.

You do not build confidence by being arrogant. You do not build confidence by being boastful. You do not build confidence by being deceptive. You build confidence by believing in yourself.

Success Is Worth the Chase

One day, all these early mornings and late nights will pay off. One day, everything you have been working toward will become a reality. Success does not come to those who wait; it comes to those who go out and get it. You may be having a tough time pulling through, or maybe right now it does not seem like there is anything to show for all the efforts you are making. But believe this: success is worth the chase. You do not have to be the best today to keep pushing. Your strength to continue does not come from being Superman in your own eyes. You just have to believe that every second counts and every step you take is important. Consistency is key; you do not stop after you have accomplished your goal or seized your dreams, or it all may slip away. As it says in 2 Timothy 2:5-6, "No one wins an athletic contest without obeying the rules. And farmers who work hard are the first to eat what grows in their field." If you want to feast upon your success, you must keep chasing.

To reach your maximum potential in life, you need to go beyond your limits, you need to give everything, and you have got to act beyond emotions. At times, your emotions will be necessary, as they are the core of your motivation that will drive you to make some difficult moves. But when emotion becomes a limitation, you will need strong will and determination. You must always be acting in interest of your future, of what will come, instead of bending to the whims of the moment.

Chapter Two
MINDSET

Trust in the Lord with all your heart, and lean not on your own understanding;
—Book of Proverbs

If you can believe, all things are possible to him who believes.
—Book of Mark

I choose to believe the Bible means exactly what it says. If every issue of life flows from the heart, then the heart is the greatest asset any man could have.

One major obsession I had as a young man was understanding how people handle failures and disappointment. It got so intense that I set aside time to study people, to wrap my head around how they could bounce back. Like, how on Earth are you able to deal with this? How did Edison find the motivation to keep inventing after ten thousand prototypes of the light bulb? How does my neighbor fail to secure a job after a year of searching and still apply to positions every single day? How can it be so easy to move on from such messes? Well, I got my answer soon enough: it all depends on mindset.

Your Mindset Is Powerful

As a young researcher, Carol Dweck performed a study in which several children were given a series of puzzles. All she wanted to know was how they would respond to complications. The first puzzles were easy to solve, so they did not have many difficulties figuring them out. But the next ones were a bit more difficult. They took the kids through some physical and mental pressure. While they toiled and moiled, the researcher kept a close watch, expecting to see them give up on the whole thing. But then, something happened.

One of the children cried out like one who just won a lottery, *"I love this, I love a challenge,"* and another added, *"You know, I was hoping this would be informative!"* Wait, what? These kids actually loved failure. Failure is something most of us dread, something we try and cope with. But here were younglings who'd found failure something to revel in. Quite bizarre! This singular experience was enough to make the kids Carol's role models, because it was clear they knew something that she probably didn't. They knew that there would always be a chance of getting better if they did not quit trying. They were not only unmoved by their failures; they never saw them as anything but growth. For them, the puzzle encounter was a learning phase. That is the power of mindset.

The actions and inactions of a man are largely determined by what goes on in his mind. Think positive and you'll most likely end up content. The view you adopt for yourself deeply affects the way you lead your life. Whether you would be the kind of person you want to be and whether you would attain the heights you admire are determined by what you fix your mind on. You cannot think of misfortune and get a fortune. What you conceive is what you achieve.

Two Types of Mindsets

There are two basic mindsets we can navigate life with, according to Carol Dweck: fixed and growth. No successful man lives life with a fixed mindset. If you believe your qualities can never be altered, you will spend your entire life trying to live up to them. People with fixed mindsets are more concerned about staying true to who they think they are than learning from mistakes and moving on with life.

Dweck explores this in her book, *Mindset: The New Psychology of Success*. In her words: "If you have only a certain amount of intelligence, a certain personality, and a certain moral character—well, then you'd better prove that you have a healthy dose of them. It simply wouldn't do to look or feel deficient in these most basic characteristics."

There are lots of people out there who are burning with the desire to prove themselves. They will stop at nothing to convince themselves and others that they are a royal flush, even though they are secretly bothered about what they really are—a pair of tens. This is evidence of a fixed mindset.

On the other hand, there is the growth mindset. The growth mindset is based on the belief that your basic qualities can always be cultivated through your own efforts. If you think you are great, why not become greater?

A man with a growth mindset accepts his flaws. He does not care about hiding them; all he desires is to overcome them. This is one step to success that most people today are not bold enough to take.

Someone once said a madman stops being mad the day he admits he is mad. Your comfort zone is not what will make you a better person; once you can break free and seek out experiences that will push your limits, you will be set for success. As Carol puts it, "The passion for stretching yourself and sticking to it, even (or especially) when it's not going well, is the hallmark of the growth mindset. This is the mindset that allows people to thrive during some of the most challenging times in their lives."

Our notions of what is risky and what is difficult come

from our mindset. While some people know what it means to challenge themselves and pursue growth, some do not give two hoots about what could happen—they run from effort like cowards, thinking the outcome will not be worth the labor. So, even though it comes as a very painful experience, don't see failure as a definition of your self-worth. Failure is a problem to face, deal with, and learn from.

The Power of "Yet"

I am so glad I found Carol's research on mindsets. One of her most compelling pieces was focused on a high school, where if students did not pass a course, they got the grade "Not Yet" instead of the conventional "Failed." It was an excellent way to change perspective on failure.

When you approach life with the mindset of "Not Yet," the hope of a better future and a successful end becomes clearer. No, this is not fantasy! There is a big difference between mere figment and fervent hope. When you are on the long road of trial and tribulation, putting one foot in front of the other is grueling. But when you refuse to stop, when you insist on treading that path, the concept of "Not Yet" will inspire you to keep moving.

There is great responsibility with this phenomenon. Do not become frustrated with "Not Yet" when you are not even ready for success to arrive.

The difference is just a word, but you already know how powerful words are. That single syllable is enough to make a difference. It builds greater confidence and gives you a course into a future that produces greater results.

Developing a Positive Mindset

Most bookstores these days are stuffed with *"secrets to success"* and *"rags to riches"* tales. We read them and feel impressed. Some of us even feel challenged and get motivated. But at the end of the day, all we get is someone spinning yarn. There is nothing to show us how to get from where we're currently stalled to where these people have ended up. Disappointingly, the inspiration we garner from reading the books only lasts a week or two, and then it is all gone.

The problem is, we are not told the right things, such as how to change our mindsets. The mind is the fountain from which every success flows. If you want to live your life with the right inspiration and sustain your drive for success, change your mindset.

A positive mind is a powerful mind, and with your mind in the right frame, you can achieve so much with your life. It is all about seeing the best in yourself, as much as you see so in others, and building the courage to pursue success until all your dreams become a reality.

When you're exploring avenues to better yourself, starting a new, healthy habit is far easier and more natural than trying to stop all your bad ones. It's a different methodology that tends to produce better results, in my experience and in that of my peers. Don't forget to celebrate small wins along the way. This is super important for those who are intentional about developing a positive mind. Celebrating small wins is recognizing your little efforts and appreciating them. Stop thinking you are not doing enough. Stop assuming your efforts are insignificant. You are putting in the effort. All you need is consistency.

Now, here is the balance: Do not consider your success a god you worship day and night. Be ready to bury your good when your better shows up. And no matter how grand, be willing to give up your better for the best. Let's say you win the lottery. What a great feat! Celebrate your win, but don't linger in the extravagant mindset. Those who win the lottery are likely to lose everything and find themselves back at ground zero within a year unless they save and invest.

There are times when nothing seems to add up. When you just need to take a break from trying so hard, and consider giving up completely. Motivation might be lost, and inspiration might seem far away from you. But there's hope.

When your heart is overwhelmed, and troubles seem like they will not end, hold on to your vision and trust in your dreams because, truly, they are valid. If you need to seek inspiration from the outside, read quotes that inspire you, meditate on Scriptures that strengthen your soul, and do not hesitate. Baby steps and short breaths; even the tiniest forward momentum is still progress.

God's Mindset

You read that right. I am talking about the one who created the universe. And the logic is quite simple: God made man in His image and after His likeness. Man has a mind. It then follows that God has a mind. If God has a mind, what would He be thinking? Does He have thoughts like men do? Does He have a cause to worry at all? Is He ever worried that the dust He breathed life into is now turning into a beast?

Well, let us see. As Prophet Jeremiah writes in Jeremiah 29:11, *"For I know the thoughts that I think toward you, says the Lord, thoughts of peace and not of evil, to give you a future and a hope."*

Let us reason together. The world has gone so crazy; senseless crimes and murder are on the rise. Yet, God is calm; His thoughts are peaceful, His mindset is positive. God created man to dominate and, of course, to bring pleasure to Him—those are the goals and the definition of success, as far as creation is concerned. But now, it looks like the whole plan is failing. Man is not dominating, and God is not pleased. Yet, God thinks of peace. This is how He wins—His mindset.

For God, it is all about the end. God is the best role model anyone could have.

Are your plans failing? Your efforts do not seem like they are any good? Your good is not good enough? Just take a deep breath. And, like God, think of peace. God has a mind and mindset. He feels disappointed, just as we do, when people go against His plans for them. But His mind is focused, set on the goal: making men just like Him. And He will stop at nothing to achieve this. Learn from God.

Your Dreams Are Valid

Your dreams are valid! Don't be discouraged. Joseph had a dream, but it made no sense to anyone. The problem was not with the dream; it was with the people. He could have just kicked the idea of greatness and all that his dream represented to the curb and moved on with the crumbs of his life. But he did not, because his aspirations were valid. Your dreams do not have to appeal to anyone in your circle. Others do not have to believe in them. Just keep pushing.

Jasmine Diane wrote on her blog an article titled "Your Dreams Are Valid." In it, she said, "We all want to fit in and be well liked, but as people we are not like cookie cutters with built-in shapes, dreams, or knowledge, instead [sic], we are more original like snowflakes that sparkle in the sunlight." Often, we are tempted to doubt our dreams or discard them totally because of what people think about them. We want to believe all others tell us. But have you ever wondered why no one sees what you see? I mean, you sleep at night, and you have dreams, literally. You wake up in the morning to narrate what you saw, but no one seems to get it. It is because the dream is yours. You saw it; you experienced it. Do not judge your dreams by other people's opinions.

Again, your dreams are valid. You may have to work a little harder and negotiate a little smarter than the person next to you, but that doesn't imply your dreams are less worthy. You are simply you. God, in His wisdom, created us as different beings. So, do not be scared to follow your dreams. Your success is tied to them.

Joseph's story is one to learn from. He was quite young and this was enough of a reason for his parents to discount him. Age can be one of the biggest challenges to overcome when trying to live out your dreams. We may feel like we can never reach a great height because we have missed our "window of opportunity" or that we cannot exceed our station until we have been around the block long enough to get some respect. You can imagine what Joseph thought when his "dreams" landed him in a pit. And as if that was not horrible enough, he was sent to prison later on.

Challenges or not, you must trust and believe that your dreams are always genuine. Time is not a hindrance; it is only a builder. Time builds you into someone who can handle those dreams and thrive with them.

Fear is a dream-killer. God gave you the spirit of power and that of a sound mind, not fear. What fear seeks to achieve is to turn your eyes upon the unknown and keep you in perpetual worry. But the way out is faith. Keep believing, keep dreaming, and do not stop moving. Sooner or later, your dreams will come true, simply because they are valid.

Create Your Vision

Your vision is important. We all have dreams in life—or, at least, we all should. But the best way to make your dreams come true is to create a powerful vision of achieving them. What you behold is what you become. This principle has its roots in the Bible, and it is ever-potent. In 2 Corinthians 3:18, Apostle Paul writes, *"But we all, with open face beholding as in a glass the glory of the Lord, are changed into the same image from glory to glory,* even *as by the Spirit of the Lord."* There are a whole lot of lessons in there. You are changed into what you set your mind upon. And that is the power of vision.

The more detail you build into your vision, the more it becomes a force to drive you towards accomplishment. Your focus on your dream is just as important as the dream itself. Like a photographer, you need to constantly adjust the lens of your mind and fix your gaze on your dream so that the end will be just perfect. When you craft your vision and hold it with your will, you begin to attract to yourself the things required for its fulfillment.

Visions remain vague until they are pinned down. Writing your vision helps your heart focus. When a vision is made plain, the hunt for it is always on your mind. Instead of moving to and fro like a caged lion, your heart can zero in on what it wants and pursue it vigorously.

I know exactly how it feels to be disparaged. There were times when every aspiration I had looked more like a fantasy than a goal to be actualized. It felt as though I was stuck in the belly of misfortune and the attention of Hell was directly on me. Worse still, I was familiar with my confusion and comfortable in my bedlam. I thought I could control it, that I didn't need to slow down or seek direction. I thought I could handle it all. But I failed. Yes, I did. It took some horrible experiences for me to realize how detached I was from my dreams. I had journeyed far away, like a prodigal son from his father's house. I knew I had to retrace my steps and realign with my vision. So, I did.

I will tell you how this happened.

I took time out to sit and reflect on my resolution years ago.

I once decided to pursue graduate education. I had made a resolution to study hard and, of course, finish as the best student in the class. Time passed and things changed. I lost focus and moved away from my goals. I was probably not finding the right motivation or I wasn't sure I wanted to keep moving. So, I took my pen and scribbled down my thoughts. I made my vision plain and wrote down my plans. And that was it! The boom was massive. I saw it play out right before my eyes—the progress, the success, and everything in between.

There is no magic here, nothing supernatural at all. It is just the power of focus. Writing brings clarity; clarity aids focus. Moving those ideas from your mind to paper creates a pictorial representation of what is to come. In this case, your writing *"is the substance of things hoped for, the evidence of things not seen"* (Hebrews 11:1).

The more attention you give to your vision, the more faith you develop in your dreams. It is not enough that you have your goals written down in some stately notepad on your bookshelf; you need to behold them until they are real to your mind. Writing down your thoughts and goals offers a bit of distance so you can sort your emotional ties and see the path; you are able to break down steps into a formal plan. You need to go over what you have written every day and remind yourself what you want regularly. Just as Rome was not built in a day, your dreams will not come true in a flash.

Truth be told, you might not like the process. In fact, you might feel like modifying your dream because it seems so unrealistic. You may think your standards are too high, or that the dream's too far against current trends. But do not let this doubt take hold. It only looks unrealistic because of where you currently are. The world will be a better place if we all stick to our vision and defy every odd we encounter. As a collective, we can band together to make the world a more inspiring, engaging place with opportunities for all.

Visualizing Your Future

In the words of Jack Canfield, "Visualization—or the act of creating compelling and vivid pictures in your mind—may be the most underutilized success tool you possess..." The ability to see your future as you want it to be stirs your subconscious mind's creative powers and lays a patch for the achievement of success. Canfield also says it helps your brain maintain focus: "Visualization focuses your brain by programming its *reticular activating system* (RAS) to notice available resources that were always there but were previously unnoticed." Research has shown that the human brain processes visualized activities like it would those performed in real life. This means that what you process in your mind is just as real to your brain as what actually physically occurs.

Visualization brings your future closer to you and helps you achieve more. You can ask Jack Nicklaus, the legendary golfer who has over one hundred tournament victories to his name. He, like many other professional athletes, applies this principle and it works perfectly for him. On one occasion, he said: "I never hit a shot, even in practice, without having a very sharp, in-focus picture of it in my head. It's like a color movie. First I see the ball where I want it to finish, nice and white and sitting up on the bright green grass. Then the scene quickly changes and I see the ball going there: its path, trajectory, and shape, even its behavior on landing. Then there's a sort of fade-out and the next scene shows me making the kind of swing that will turn the previous images into reality…" That is exactly how visualization works. You see what you want, and eventually, you get what you see.

This isn't some magic answer. It can be so frustrating to be able to perfectly imagine what you want, yet know that your reality is far from it. The conflict can feel so intense. But your subconscious mind will try to bring a resolution by transforming your current life into the vision you have.

Visualization, for athletes, is called "mental rehearsal." They dedicate a few minutes to this process and repeat it every day. All they do is imagine a flawless performance and rehearse it in their minds, without any physical movement whatsoever. And this way, they improve behavioral performance, cognitive thinking patterns, and internal states. Now, that shouldn't stop you from pushing yourself. It should not make you strive less. It should only be a drive to do more.

Most successful people in the world today see their dreams as already achieved mentally and spiritually. You should too. But while you're at it, do not neglect the gift of today. After visualizing each goal and seeing it as complete, let go and live in the present moment.

Your Mindset Affects Your Vision; Your Vision Affects Your Mindset

Now, this a bit tricky. But to make it clear and relatable, let us pause. Think about all you have read in this book in the last few minutes. Then, breathe. How have the lessons in this book affected you? Have you noticed any changes in your thinking patterns? Does it feel like you have been seeing things differently? If you answered in the affirmative, then you would agree with me: *your mindset and your vision are intertwined.* What you see influences what you think, and what you think determines what you see. If I head right out of my house, stand in the middle of the garden, and look upon the hot, remorseless sun for too long, chances are high that I would see its reflection on everything I set my eyes on after.

Success is not an accident. To change your mindset and see the future just as you desire it to be, you need to change your vision. Your mind is hyper-concentrated on what your eyes see throughout the day. Have you ever had nightmares about something shocking you've seen during the day—like a scary movie or a huge roach, maybe? Exactly. That's the power of sight and mindset. Your sight shapes your thought patterns. Feast your eyes with the right things, and in no time, you will begin to develop the growth mindset that is necessary for success.

Once you can define a clearer outlook on where you want to be in the future, and consciously build a vision that keeps you on track, it is important to maintain a positive mindset so that you do not throw in the towel. The right mindset helps you to grow and learn along the journey. It keeps you firm and unwavering. Even when you encounter misfortune, you will stay the course and endure the process.

It is not as easy as it seems on paper, but it is achievable. Remember that the best things in life are often hard-won.

Every day is a new opportunity to grow and learn. If you ask me, the greatest thing you can give to a man is an opportunity for growth. Having a growth mindset allows you to see your situation to its end. It gives you the perception of a sojourner who sees the destination of the journey rather than the potholes along the way.

The decision to keep moving is yours to make. When

tribulations come and troubles abound, get up, and say, "I am not going back. I will learn from this."

THE ACTIONS
AND INACTIONS
OF A MAN
ARE LARGELY
DETERMINED
BY WHAT GOES
ON IN HIS MIND.

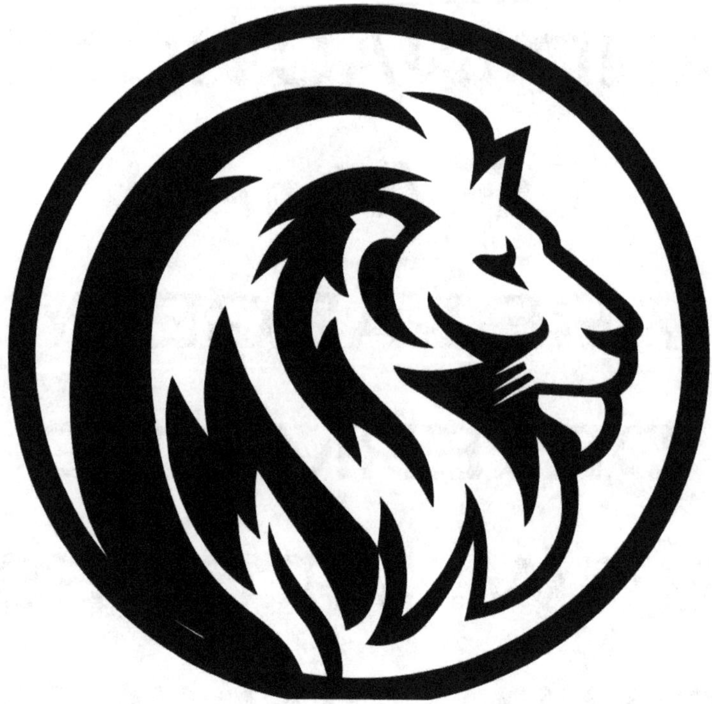

Chapter Three
BELIEF SYSTEM

For as he thinks in his heart, so is he.
—Book of Proverbs

But when you ask, you must believe and not doubt because the one who doubts is like a wave of the sea, blown and tossed by the wind.
—Book of James

I'll start off by quoting the words of José Ortega y Gasset, a Spanish philosopher and essayist who worked during the first half of the 20th century while Spain dangled between monarchy, republicanism, and dictatorship:

"In beliefs we live, we move, and we are...the beliefs constitute the base of our life, the land on which we live... All our conduct, including the intellectual life, depends on the system of our authentic beliefs. In them...lies latent, as implications of whatever we do or

we think...the man, at heart, is believing or, which is equal, the deepest stratum of our life, the spirit that maintains and carries all the others, is formed by beliefs..."

It is a common fact that we are social animals, and that we develop by interacting with the people around us. But the community of humans is far beyond that of an animal herd. We create societies and develop structures based on beliefs. Our belief systems are what make us different. And they truly determine the decisions we make and the habits we develop.

In simple words, your belief system is your notion about what is right and wrong, or what is true and false; it's an ideology or set of principles that influence your interpretation of everyday reality.

Our level of success in life is tied to our system of belief. To thrive on an upward swing and make steady progress, you need to see life the right way and judge situations with the proper standards. A few years ago, I came across a young man who never believed in making it big. For him, "Life is a bunch of coincidences. Success is all about being lucky. It is either you are destined for it, or you are not. No amount of labor could get a man to the top if he weren't made for it." Those were his utterances. And, yes, I was shocked to my very core. Nothing he said was correct. But he already had that belief system. And that would determine what befell him over time. Life is no coincidence. Life is intentional because God is. Success is not a thing of luck. It is a reward of labor and diligence. Recall God said to Joshua, the son of Nun: *"This book of the law shall not depart out of thy mouth; but thou shalt meditate therein day and night, that thou mayest observe to do according to all that is written therein: for then thou shalt make thy way prosperous, and then thou shalt have good success"* (Joshua 1:8).

If you see life as evil, you will most likely experience everything evil in life. No, it is not a curse. It is a principle. Belief systems are not built overnight, just like you do not mature in a single day. It takes ideas, notions, and sometimes experiences to develop a belief system. When you feed on the right things, you will get the right beliefs.

How Beliefs Are Formed

Our beliefs are like our subconscious autopilot. Once formed, they become part of us; we begin to navigate life by their dictations and make decisions from their influence.

But how exactly are they formed? Here is an example: I believe God exists. I believe He created the world and gave the mandate of procreation to man. I believe He is the reason behind every reason and the root of every success and achievement. When and how did I form this belief? I have not seen God at any time and I have not heard Him speak, not even once. But I believe He exists.

This is the trick: beliefs are formed either by experiences, inferences, deductions, or by accepting what others tell us to be true. Just like me, most believers are told about God in sermons. They hear there is a God up there who knows every man by name and has all power in Heaven and Earth, and they read about Him in books and Scripture.

Most of our core beliefs were formed when we were children. As newborn babies, we had no idea whatsoever of what existed and what did not—no preconceived notion about what was true or false. We all came into being with a clean slate. But growing up, we become so curious and impressionable. Ever wondered why your kid asks questions about almost everything? They are hungry for knowledge, eager to learn all they can about the world around them. Children like to find meaning in everything they see. In fact, they sometimes go overboard. I remember finding my ten-year-old cousin in my reading room years ago; the problem was not his being there, but his snooping.

"Hey, John! What are you doing in there?" I asked.

"Coz, I'm trying to find out what keeps you behind closed doors for hours every day," he replied, looking so serious and determined.

How was that any of his business? But kids want to know, and most times, they are sincere in their quest for knowledge.

Somehow, they come across facts, ideas, notions, and thoughts that sink deep into their mind and remain there. They want to be like the mentors around them, mimic the adults in their lives. They get exposed to aspects of the world that give them a definition of life and success. And that's how beliefs start forming.

Our parents, environment, and encounters have a big role to play when it comes to molding our beliefs. Paul said to Timothy in his Epistle, *"Remember that ever since you were a child, you have known the Holy Scriptures, which are able to give you the wisdom that leads to salvation through faith in Christ Jesus"* (2 Timothy 3:15). It was clear that Timothy's beliefs were greatly influenced by his mother, Eunice, and his grandmother, Lois, for him to have known the Scriptures from a young age.

What we are exposed to early in life is what forms our system of belief over time. If you want to get the right beliefs, watch what you expose yourself to.

The Foundation of Your Belief System

Our minds consist of two main parts—the conscious and the subconscious. According to research published by Emma Young, the subconscious mind is 95 percent responsible for responding to the external environment. On the other hand, our conscious mind is the seat of logical control, and it has a mere 5 percent role in processing the stimuli received by our senses.

Our subconscious mind creates a great portion of the beliefs we hold throughout life. These beliefs carry emotion, and emotion turns into action. Without a doubt, your belief system has the power to dictate the direction of your life, whether good or bad. It can determine the quality of the life you lead and whether you will achieve your desired success.

We all have a deep-seated need to believe in *something*. It is an instrumental function of humans as we seek community, purpose, and peace. Thus, having our belief system tampered with can cause us serious distress and emotional anguish. We often decide to stick with those beliefs like glue as a result. But there are occasions when we need to endure the pain and let go completely. Wrong belief systems can be quite *deadly*.

God knows how important it is for us to believe Him, and He mentions it repeatedly in the Bible. If at any point in your life you have felt the frustration of trying to state a truth to a group of scoffers who would rather face a firing squad than accept anything you say, you can understand (a bit) how God feels when people doubt His words.

Jesus, during His earthly ministry, constantly fought against wrong beliefs. He knew just how powerful beliefs were to the people of Jerusalem, and He made sure their faith was founded in truth and goodness. Many were loath to accept this new belief system Jesus presented them with because of their ingrained beliefs they had grown up with. As a matter of fact, some of those closest to Him rejected His message, and paid no attention to His preaching.

A great number of the errors people wind up making can be traced back to the beliefs they hold. Once you get trapped in your belief, you are likely to end up on the wrong side of fate. Beliefs are meant to be reviewed and evaluated from time to time, because our current emotions can get in the way of our perceptions and end up tainting our perspective. You almost never can tell in the moment; the way you feel today might be influenced by tough times, a half-truth you were told as a youth, or a narrow range of experience. But you are not your condition. You are not what you are going through. You are so much more, and yet, simply *you!*

It is wise to build our belief system around what we visualize instead of our current circumstances. The success you wish to achieve tomorrow will only come if you see it in your mind today and progress with the same consciousness. Do not let down your guard because you have been disappointed or feel out of sorts. Choose to believe in your dreams, and they will come true one day.

Believe It Is Possible

Now that we have established the importance of belief

systems, the question is: *what should you believe?* As simple as this question is, it is where a lot of people miss the mark. What we believe, most of the time, is what we think is true. But the truth is not dependent on our opinions.

I would say you ought to believe what you want to achieve: success. Believe that success is possible, and you will soon get it. The mind is such a powerful instrument; it can help you achieve success in everything you want. But you must believe that what you want is possible.

Jack Canfield gave a profound example of the power of belief in his book *The Success Principles*: "Doctors in Texas [...]—studying the effect of arthroscopic knee surgery—assigned patients with sore, worn-out knees to one of three surgical procedures: scraping out the knee joint, washing out the joint, or doing nothing.

"During the 'nothing' operation, doctors anesthetized the patient, made three incisions in the knee as if to insert their surgical instruments, and then pretended to operate. Two years after surgery, patients who underwent the pretend surgery reported the same amount of relief from pain and swelling as those who had received the actual treatments. The brain *expected* the 'surgery' to improve the knee, and it did."

This is not fiction. It is a real-life example. Our whole life is spent being conditioned. Neuropsychologists have found that the brain will predict changes and transformations and enact them on the body, regardless of physical interaction. This is known as the placebo effect.

Your belief is important. I cannot emphasize this enough. It is both spiritual and psychological. You need to remind yourself that success is not a myth. People succeed every day, and they are just as human as you are. No, this is not a reason to get into a rat race. It is not an attempt to make you feel bad. It is a challenge—a sincere one, at that. You need to hold positive expectations in your mind every single day. Believe that success is achievable, and go on to pursue your goals.

Identifying Limiting Beliefs

The beliefs we hold can either empower or limit us. While empowering beliefs push you forward and invoke positive thoughts, limiting beliefs bottle you up. This explains why some people thrive and make headway in the most trying times, and some do not.

A man with limiting beliefs sees the negative side of everything. His progress in life is tied to conditions, and when they are not met, he fails. You can liken such a person to the children of Israel after being freed in Egypt. They were saved from slavery, but not in their hearts. *"Why did you bring us out of Egypt, anyway?"* they questioned God and Moses. *"While we were there, didn't we tell you to leave us alone? We would rather be slaves in Egypt than die in this desert."*

Limiting beliefs highlight constraints and impossibilities. They can hinder a man from achieving success in life. To identify them, a man needs to examine what drives his actions and responses. Ask yourself questions such as, *"What is responsible for this decision I am making? Is this just about now or the future? Where does this lead to?"* When you realize your beliefs are potentially damaging to you, you know it is time to drop them. And hey, you need to be sincere with yourself here. The scary thing about beliefs is, only you know what they are. You know what you believe in and what inspires your thoughts and actions. No one else does. The best any other person can do is study your behavior and make speculations. Your beliefs are the bottom of your mind and the floor of your heart. So, the only way to point them out is to admit them sincerely. There is no harm in being wrong; the harm is in being wrong and feigning rightness. To make progress in life, you must be willing to acknowledge flaws and scorn mediocrity. Even Jesus Christ did. He cried out to the one who could save him—*God*—when it was no longer soothing to drink from His cup.

It is not enough to identify your wrong beliefs. In fact, identifying them should not depress you; it should spur you to do more and to continue educating yourself spiritually and ideologically. You are in for a long haul if you decide to slow down in order to wallow. Identifying your limiting beliefs should help you replace them and proceed on the right track.

Replacing Limiting Beliefs

Like I said, identifying detrimental beliefs is one thing; replacing them is another. This supersession must be very deliberate and genuine, of course. Do not jump at an idea because it is in vogue. A new belief is not automatically better. Swapping out your personal code for the next best thing is no way to get through life. As Alexander Hamilton is credited with saying, "Those who stand for nothing fall for anything." Reflect deeply on how changing your beliefs will affect every aspect of your existence.

There are times I literally get lost in reflection. I get myself out of the noise, into a place of solitude and calmness, and then I mull over life and what it means to truly live. Mind you, to live here is not merely to exist. It is deeper than that. During those times, I realize things I had never understood about myself; I can see success in an entirely new light.

So, take a pause and reflect genuinely. You will find a notion, or two, that you have held for too long, and which has held you back and made you static. For example, thoughts like *"Nobody should be trusted; everyone is the same"* will cause you to be unnecessarily suspicious. And you might begin to close yourself off from those who are supposed to push you forward and help you attain your dreams. The worst part is, you will have no one to share your problems with. No man is an island of his own. If all humans are the same, then you should not be trusted either.

Once you identify such deadly beliefs, think of real-life examples that prove them wrong. If you have always believed that all humans are the same and no one should be trusted, think about times when you trusted in someone who did not let you down. Chances are, you will find one, but consider other people's experiences if you do not. Someone around you must have trusted in someone who eventually came through.

Now that you have proved your belief wrong and officially deemed it unworthy, allow the evidence to sink deep—meditate on it till your mind knows and believes it. This is not a one-day occurrence. It is not something you chew upon for a couple of days and then neglect. You need to silence the voice of your former thoughts and make sure they are never heard again. Remember, your limiting beliefs were not formed in a day. It took weeks, or even years, of exposure to form wrong notions and ideas. So, you need to be more deliberate this time. Change is never achieved all at once. Think and feel the right beliefs in your core, and you will soon forget all that you previously held to be true.

I must add here that your new beliefs will eventually change your perception about life and cause you to act differently. If you never trusted anyone before, you will probably start noticing the admirable traits of those around you and be more open to those who are willing to help now. Hey, make no mistake! Not all humans can be trusted. Therefore, our beliefs must be reviewed and always checked.

Right Belief Systems for Success

Someone once said there are no right or wrong beliefs, only beliefs that limit or empower you. Well, while this is not entirely false, I consider this concept in itself to be a belief that can limit or empower.

If you believe there are no absolute rights or wrongs for belief systems, you might be driven to make the best out of every given scenario. For example, I believe *"Opportunities come but once,"* yet I don't consider this entirely right or wrong. Therefore, when opportunities arise I carefully select those that are most appealing and do not let the engaging ones slip. I don't need to make a mad grab at whatever chances appear because it's not as if opportunities will never be available again.

Regardless, we all can consciously instill some deep beliefs inside ourselves to help us achieve our dreams. Yes, there are right beliefs we have all got to have, and when I call them *"right,"* you know what I mean—empowering thought patterns, philosophies of living that enhance growth and success, and the like. To get what we genuinely want, we must believe the right things. Our realities in life are created and sustained by our beliefs. Whether we are aware of them or not, they affect us.

So, the first belief I firmly stand by is that of *possibility*. I have said this earlier, but I will say it again: If you do not believe you can do something, you are probably not going to attempt it. And even if you do, you will be unable to pursue it with all your competency and potential. What you believe will either expand or limit you. So, believe your dreams are achievable.

What do you hold as true in the deepest part of your heart? Or what should you believe in to achieve your desired success? Growing up, I had friends who would rather work with what was on the ground than open their minds to the possibilities. When I would talk about my dreams, they would laugh me to scorn and "advise" me to be honest with myself.

I knew I was on the right path; I knew I had to visualize my dreams and view them as achievable. But somehow, I started doubting. And that was it. Doubting cost me some level of progress. I could not stand my ground in that moment, and it was my greatest undoing ever. Dear reader, *believe in yourself*, believe in your dreams. Believe you can achieve success, and you will never be too small to get the ball rolling.

Believing in yourself is trusting that you have the right stuff.

It helps you see your abilities and not your inabilities. It gives you the confidence you need to keep moving. And like a lion in the grasslands, you can face everything and anything that comes your way.

I must be clear on what believing in yourself is *not*. It isn't overconfidence. It is not pure independence, meaning it is not boastful. Come on, no one gets to the top all by himself. I really have never heard of anyone who got up there without the influence of a single person, at the very least. The truth is, you need help! God created humans to be social beings. So, I would advise you trash every thought of independence and learn to relate with others.

Let us talk about another belief necessary for success—the belief that there's *room for growth*, always. By now, I trust you understand that your beliefs shape your reality. So, you need to watch your beliefs. If you desire growth, believe there is an opportunity to grow at every turn. No circumstance or challenge is difficult enough to make you stop growing. Sounds hard, but it's true. Whether you see it or you do not, opportunities abound. And they can always be created. While one man sees a coronavirus pandemic as a serious disaster that hinders progress, another man considers it an opportunity to explore new possibilities. The hindrance only exists in your head. Those who do not think anything good can come out of Nazareth will never see it when it eventually comes. Do not underestimate the power of your beliefs.

Ultimately, *believe in God.* God is real. And it is impossible to receive from Him without believing. Why? *Because anyone who wants to approach Him must believe both that He exists and that He cares enough to reward those who seek Him* (Hebrews 11:6). God is good, and every good thing you hear about Him is true. But He demands that we believe Him in order to receive all things good from Him. It is quite simple. If you do not believe I can give you what you want, why come to me for it? I believe. It is a cause-and-effect thing. It's a principle that will exist till the end of time: believe, and you shall receive.

BELIEVING IN YOURSELF IS TRUSTING THAT YOU HAVE THE RIGHT STUFF. IT HELPS YOU SEE YOUR ABILITIES AND NOT YOUR INABILITIES. IT GIVES YOU THE CONFIDENCE YOU NEED TO KEEP MOVING.

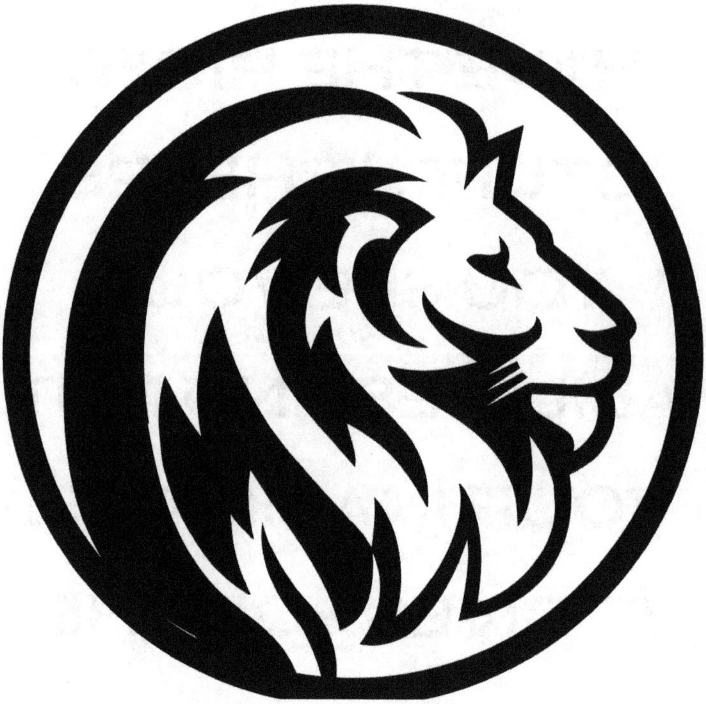

Chapter Four
PARTNERSHIPS & ASSOCIATIONS

He who walks as a companion with wise men will be wise, but the companions of fools are fools themselves.
—Book of Proverbs

Story time. John is a young, brilliant chap who succeeds at almost anything he does. He knows just how to get what he wants, and he would stop at nothing to have that ability at his disposal. No, John is not all that rich compared to most Americans; his parents are middle class and live averagely. But he has nearly all he needs to achieve his dreams.

By good luck, John gets into a higher institution at age nineteen. And the tide turns. He makes friends with the worst students—the ones who love extreme pleasure, couldn't care less about being diligent, and have no clear-cut direction for life. John never really planned this. He never thought he would end up in the company of such people. He never saw himself as one who could be easily swayed. But it happened anyway. John's peers make him want to explore the world of frivolities. He begins to live and act like his new "friends" and his dreams no longer mean anything to him.

So, what went wrong? A lot! John was not able to stand his ground, and the pressure got too overwhelming.

We all want to be successful; we all want to make it in life. But are we all willing to pay the price? Maybe not. If you are ever going to get success, you must flock with the right people.

Associations do matter. The idea that the people you spend time with have nothing to do with what you want to achieve is the biggest lie that could possibly be told. Do not be fooled. You need to surround yourself with those who are on the same path as yours and those who have accomplished the goals you seek.

Who you become is, to a large extent, dependent on who you hang out with. Parents understand this, and that's why you hear things like, *"I don't want to see you go close to those kids,"* or the classic *"Would you jump off a cliff because your friend did?"* growing up. No, Mom and Dad were not wicked, as we thought in our youth. They only knew better—they'd learned that the company you keep matters. They have had true-life experiences, and they know how influential peer pressure can be. So, they chose to be hard on you rather than watch you go down the drain. Truly, no discipline seems pleasant at the time. Later, however, it produces a harvest of peace for those trained by it. Whether you realize it or not, the people you look up to have control over your actions.

Who Do You Associate With?

I have come to realize that associates are not something to take lightly. The decision of who to move forward with must be taken seriously if you are ever going to land your desired success. According to a saying made popular by Jim Rohn, "You are the average of the five people you spend the most time with." Have you ever wondered why couples sound alike, or both partners act in a unique manner, after living together? Well, it is the power of association.

Humans are social beings—I have said this before, and I am saying it again. When you surround yourself with the wrong influences, you are bound to conform to their reality and align your standards with theirs. This is not exactly spiritual. There is a bit of science in it. Heather R. Walen of San Diego State University and Margie E. Lachman of Brandeis University once conducted a study about the positive and negative side effects of various relationships. They got down to brass tacks the effect of different bonds on patients' stress levels. A participant whose social relationship was perceived to be negative was likely to have his or her stress hormones elevated to a level higher than normal.

Also, several other research types have been conducted to prove that negative relationships can negatively impact human actions.

Now, to be clear, your associations are not merely those who are around you. I mean, not everyone in your place of work can be classified as your associate. The mere fact that you relate with them does not mean they fall under this category. Here is what I am saying: you cannot always be around those who are as purposeful as you are. But you can seek to spend quality time with those who motivate you, inspire you, and want the same things you do. Remember, the decision is yours to make.

Let's talk about peer pressure. I understand what it means to be the "odd one out," because I have been there. Finding yourself in an environment where no one seems to see the world as you see it or understand what you do can be frustrating, especially if you are not secure in your beliefs. In fact, forget being secure; even the toughest folks get caught in peer pressure. But your true friends won't pressure you to give up your dreams, and as long as you truly believe in yourself, no amount of coercion will bring you off your path. Take comfort in the fact that no test or temptation is beyond what others have had to face.

When you learn to maintain focus early in life, you will have no problem dealing with pressures around you. Focus helps you see just one thing at times where there's so much to look at. Focus helps you stay determined and persistent about what you want, and block out everything arbitrary. Focus helps you say "No" when you need to and "Yes" when necessary.

Flee From Every Appearance of Evil

One major mistake we make in life is waiting to be adversely affected before learning a lesson. Who said you must be the foul-up? Who said you must be shot in the foot before learning to be wary of stray bullets? Rather than waiting to be struck so you can find a cure for your ailment, why not do away with all that can cause you illness?

Unfortunately, bad associations are difficult to recognize at the start. Even Satan himself masquerades as an angel of light. Those who seem like potential friends may only wish to sway you, or harm you. Sometimes, they will seem like the exact people you need to roll with. But hey! Be guided and fully guarded. Once you notice inconsistency and dissimilarity, flee!

Yes, it might not be so easy to break ties with peers, especially when you have gotten so used to their company. But does it matter? You know what you want and where you are heading, so flee. This might seem a little bit elementary, but trust me, it is not. The right solution is often the simplest. People who constantly complain and doubt every dream you have are not a good fit for you, and keeping them around can be disastrous. The words they speak can subtly creep into your mind and form a belief that may limit you forever, if you cannot find the strength to dismantle it. Do not sacrifice your dreams on the altar of relationships; instead, distance yourself from such people and seek the right influences.

The Framingham Heart Study, which kicked off in 1948, has shown that emotions can be contagious. From the thousands of data samples (both social and medical) collected, it was proven that "each happy friend a person associated with increased their chances of personal happiness by 11%." But sadness and negativity appeared to be more infectious: "for every sad individual a person associated with, their chances of being unhappy were doubled." Now you see where the problem lies. You cannot surround yourself with toxic and negative people and expect not to be affected. The contact with defeatist mindsets will alter how you react to future events and circumstances. And just like Raphael Collazo states in his article, *The Power of Association — Who Do You Associate With?*, "Prolonged exposure to stress compromises the effectiveness of neurons in the hippocampus and can permanently damage neural pathways, inhibiting your ability to think clearly, reason effectively, and develop memories."

Before they become a stronghold, get rid of every relationship that can be regarded as toxic. It is easier to uproot a plant than to dig up a tree. You have nothing to lose by giving up toxic relationships; you are only making room for more successful associations and healthy relationships.

Before Partnering

Naturally, you want to go all out and build a team for yourself. You want to partner with friends who would help your dreams come true and give you the right motivations for success. You want to jump at every chance to get closer to the best so you can be identified with great people. All good. But just before you step out of your shell, guard yourself and stay focused on your core genius. It was Malcolm S. Forbes that opined, "Success follows doing what you want to do. There is no other way to be successful."

It is so rare to find those who have the same values and dreams as you do, and once these rare folk enter your life, it's these relationships you should cherish. They are the prime people to choose as partners, for you both can experience a lifetime of inspiration and support. As the saying goes, *"If you want to go fast, go alone; but if you want to go far, go together."* Forging a path with someone at your side will help you build confidence in your pursuit. At your low moments, when it seems like there is no way forward, your chosen group will pat you on the back and keep you motivated.

However, you need to see success in yourself first. Successful people do not see themselves as failures. If you do not see yourself as someone who has potential or can handle success, partnering might be the worst decision to make. You ought to be giving as much as you get. Imagine you have little or no drive—you refuse to go out of your comfort zone or offer total commitment. You'd have major issues going into a partnership with someone who's full of zeal and a passion for exploring. Be sure you have what it takes to mingle with successful minds. Don't just aim to get value; give value yourself.

While I was in Los Angeles on a short break, I met some young folks who asked me to partner with them on a project that aimed to kick-start a clothing brand. At first, I was taken by surprise at the level of boldness they had. These guys had barely known me for two months; I was merely an older friend they met during a concert. But, I engaged them in a conversation, and what got my attention was how much effort they had put into the project already. Not only that, but these folks also mapped out plans that I probably could not have stumbled upon if I was in their shoes. And it was quite impressive. Without thinking twice, I agreed on a partnership, and we hit the ground running. Trust me, the clothing brand project ranked as one of the most successful achievements I had that year.

Now, this is the lesson I learned from that experience: success is achieved in partnership when both parties have something to offer; not just something, in fact, but something worthwhile. I would not have given an ear to whatever proposal they had if they were all about getting from me. While I offered a clearer approach to the economy and the target audience, they provided the resources to enter the market.

For a partnership to work well and achieve the desired success, it must be solid. Solid partnerships are the ones with enough resources, including time and energy, from both ends. So, before you consider partnering, make yourself an asset.

Creating Successful Partnerships

"Personal relationships are the fertile soil from which all advancement, all success, all achievement in real life grows," said Ben Stein. After building yourself into one who can best complement another for success, what next?

I want to confirm a notion here. *Must I partner with someone? Do I need to join forces with somebody before I can conquer failure?* Oh, yes! You need someone. No matter how much you do alone, you can do much more with others.

Successful relationships are a force—the kind of force you need to remain challenged and fresh-thinking. Your best effort will not always be enough, you know. There will be times when you need an outside perspective, someone else's insight, in order to move forward. You need to have friends or family who can both empower your beliefs and call you out on your poor decisions.

The story of Larry Page and Sergey Brin, founders of Google, keeps inspiring me each time I come across it. They did not start out as friends. Truth is, they disagreed about almost everything when they first met, yet later struck a partnership. In their case, success came not because they had all key aspects at once, but because they had a select few qualities in common. This is the point I am driving at. The perfect partner is not going to be someone with all the skills and experience you desire; they will be someone you want to journey with in order to gain those features together. This is why the compatibility of your most basic instincts and perspectives is so vital. Do not expect to have a successful landing when you partner with someone whose values do not line up with yours. If I love to speak and desire to be the best public speaker that will ever live, I will not partner with a shy, reserved person. When it comes to creating relationships, what matters most is the alignment of purpose.

To create a successful relationship, consider all you would like to achieve at the end of the day, and what stands in your way. How do you need to be pushed, and how do you need to be complimented? Then, take time to study your environment and those in it—study how they react and respond to circumstances, study how they speak and what matters most to them, and study where they are heading and what spurs their actions. This might require a little bit of your time and energy. But on the road to success, you must be intentional with every step.

The Importance of Cohesion

"Can two walk together, unless they are agreed?" (Amos 3:3).

The Bible is clear on the issue of partnership. No form of partnership flourishes without agreement—even Abraham had to agree with God before entering a covenant with Him. Agreement builds and sustains every relationship, and it makes the race easy to run. When a man finds the one with whom he would love to tread the path of success, he is full of hope and optimism that someday he will get to his destination. And as beautiful as this is, it is not just said and done. One must spell out his terms and be sure that his companion is willing to submit to them. If you cannot articulate your desires and routes, then you are not ready to begin your journey to success, let alone enter a partnership. Be certain about where you are heading and why you choose to travel there with a particular person. It always helps to be straightforward and honest.

Agreement is not limited to the terms discussed before getting into a partnership; it includes how you get past hurdles in your journey. Can you develop a cohesive nature, one that teaches you to turn to each other during strife so you can tackle problems together? If all you do in your circle is lock horns and run counter to one another, it is only a matter of time before you begin to lose focus. And then, things will begin to fall apart. One person wants it done this way, another wants to do it that way, and the third? He probably has no side, so he sits on the fence. How exactly do you expect to move forward? Yes, there are bound to be arguments. But if we do not learn to put aside our differences and focus on what binds us together, we might never hit the mark.

Make Your Partnership Work

Partnerships are about so much more than the initial meeting. Sure, there are books and movies about success which offer proven, practical ways to establish partnerships. But there is more. So much more that those sources probably aren't telling you.

After you have created a successful relationship, you need to be able to manage it, and make the partnership work for you. Being in association with people with great dreams is not an automatic guarantee. What if you begin to disagree with their methods? What if you drop out or get tired along the line? *What if?* I have seen so many people who started out with such fire, such intelligence and instinct, but, for some reason or another, gave into external influences and departed.

To make your partnership work, you need trust. Trust is the

foundation of every successful relationship. This is not just about believing in your partner's eagerness; it extends to a firm reliance on their abilities and capabilities. You must be able to vouch for and believe in their judgments and all that they stand to represent. This is how success is achieved. When you trust those in your circle, you form a tough bond that pushes you both to endure—it becomes easy to be open and say things just like they are, without the fear of stepping on anyone's toes. Instead of spending time watching your back, you can focus on the dreams and vision that brought you together.

If, for instance, you are in an association of folks who sing, your efforts and energy should always be directed towards growing in the music industry—not ironing out issues between members of the team.

Beyond trust, respect is another essential for positive long-lasting partnerships. When you respect those whom you hang around and share ideas with, you value their points of view and contributions, just as they do yours. Respect is reciprocal—if you want it, give it. Respecting those you associate with helps you take their words seriously and develop better ideas at every point. No, they do not have to be much older or have better experience; they only must be people with like minds, people you look up to in one way or the other, or people whose potentials you have confidence in.

People with successful partnerships do not only accept the opinions of different people on their team; they also welcome them. It is not a question of whether A's idea or B's suggestion resonates with you at first. Welcoming diversity is a virtue, and one you should fully embrace to achieve success.

And finally, communicate! We communicate every single day. Whether you chat up the person next to you or spend the entire day sending and receiving messages on social media, communication is communication. But if you are ever going to keep your associations and make your partnership work for you, maintain effective communications. I am not suggesting you become talkative in the name of being interactive; I am only saying to speak up when you need to and make your mind plain before your team members. Do not hoard information or keep details from others because you want to outdo them or have an edge. Do not retreat from every important discussion and keep mute when your opinion is needed. The better and more effective your communication, the richer your relationships. Keep your relationship through communication, and success will be a no-brainer.

You can only sustain the success built by an association by remaining in that association.

It takes consistency to maintain what has already been built. While you are making it big with the right associations and achieving great things by their influence, remember to stay loyal and committed to the relationship. Breaking out of successful associations prematurely can be your greatest undoing; it is an act that reeks of arrogance. It's great to consistently be on the move and on to the next achievement—that's a sign of a success-driven person. However, sometimes, the right move is staying and investing in your passion projects. As long as your associations remain true and useful, it's unwise to discard them for the next star on the horizon.

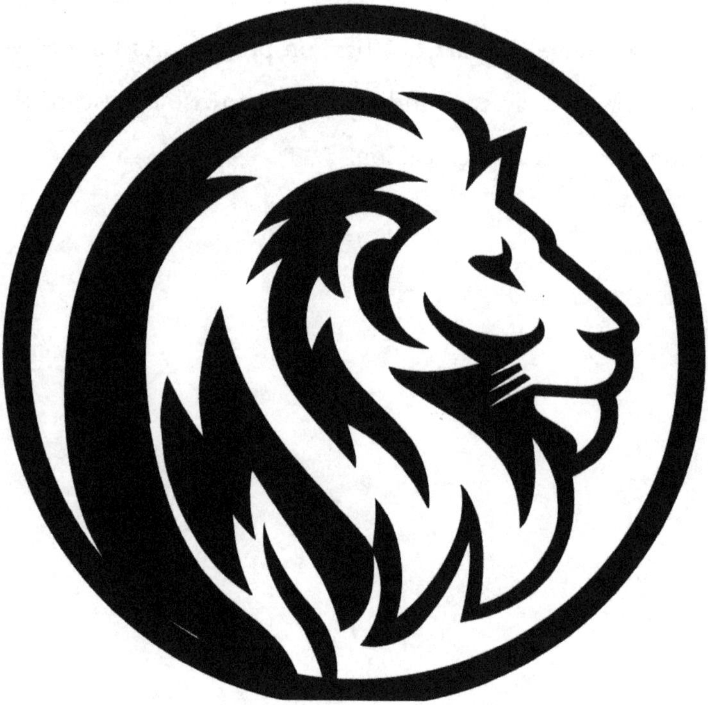

Chapter Five

DETERMINATION

I can do all things through Christ who strengthens me.
—Book of Philippians

Vince Lombardi's saying "Winners never quit, and quitters never win" is one you've probably heard before. But the fact that it is said often does not mean you have gotten a full grasp of what it is all about. Knowledge, for me, is not power; its application is. So, when you know but do not do, your knowledge is as good as not knowing. *"But be doers of the word, and not hearers only…"* (James 1:22).

Call it determination, courage, or whatever you like, but the will to keep moving is a necessary ingredient of success. Repeatedly, history has proven that no man can get to the top of the ladder without having the will to do so. I remember watching a two-year-old lad climb up the stairs a few years ago. Despite the falls, he never stopped rising and moving. And yes, it took over an hour, but he got up there.

According to research conducted by Carol Dweck, the importance of determination outweighs that of intelligence. For a study that put smarts vs. grit to the test, Dweck's team gave a group of kids a series of puzzles to solve. Half were praised for their effort, while the other half was praised for being smart.

The kids could choose the kind of test they wanted to take second; they could either take a more difficult test than the first, or one that was easier. And here's where being praised for raw intelligence failed. A great portion of the kids praised for being smart opted for the easier test while the tenacious ones chose to deal with the more difficult puzzles.

Your intelligence and other natural abilities are innately passive, but determination is not—it is much more active. This means that even though your innate talents create opportunities for you, you need actions to make them work. Intelligence can land you a job, but determination helps you stay committed.

Determination is all about maintaining focus and defying odds. Once you have a set goal, you keep moving and growing until you get to the peak. You do not have to be the best yet; with determination, you can climb any mountain.

The "I Can" Attitude

Elizabeth Ferguson, or "Liz," was a perfectly normal young lady who suddenly fell ill with leukemia. She lost everything she had—her health, job, money, all gone! Her health got so bad that nothing could be done to remedy it. As told on her website, "[The doctors] said I would probably be sick for quite a long time, but they couldn't say for how long or even if I would ever recover."

After a year spent struggling to perform even the most basic tasks, Liz managed to find the strength to start working on her laptop for brief periods of time a day. After another six months of recovery, she was able to start making YouTube videos from her home.

Her health gradually continued to improve, and her business—a website and YouTube channel for International English Language Testing System (IELTS) preparation—gained popularity. It seemed like things were getting back in shape, and her life was going to get better after all. Little did she know, her troubles were not over.

Two and half years into her battle with leukemia, her health suddenly deteriorated again. It was crushing for her. Worst of all, her own family's support dwindled. Liz stated, "I felt deep despair at this time. [...] I ended up living completely alone while still being sick, disabled and unable to walk outside."

But she never gave up.

Liz became successful in the end—not just successful, but remarkably successful. If having over a million subscribers on her YouTube channel (@IELTS Liz) and one of the most popular websites for IELTS preparation in the world while dealing with years of illness and hardships is not success, I wonder what is. Liz was a tutor who poured her heart into her job while battling leukemia. But she never let it defeat her.

The key is determination. The odds were obviously against Liz, but she remained determined and focused. Having the "I Can" attitude helps you stay positive and resolute. Tough times or not, you will always pursue your goal, knowing full well that it is achievable.

A huge part of the "I Can" attitude is not allowing for negative perspectives to cloud your mind. To ensure this, you have to do away with complaining. When you stumble, make mistakes, it's fine to voice your frustration and find an outlet for your emotions, but you cannot wallow. You cannot let yourself be lost in whining and declarations of how unfair life is and how you don't understand why things are the way they are. This will poison your mentality and pull you away from the focused attitude you need to embrace further challenges and learn to grow.

Do Not Fear Learning New Things!

The fear of knowledge, I would say, is the beginning of failure.

Successful people do not stop learning—they learn while they are full and while they are empty, while they are good and while they are bad, while they are high and while they are low. *"The discerning heart seeks knowledge, but the mouth of a fool feeds on folly,"* so the Bible says (Proverbs 15:14).

When you are determined to have success, you are willing to go any length to get it. Learning new ideas and developing new skills help you see beyond where you currently are and explore new possibilities you never knew existed. So, while you are willing to learn new things, be cautious of what you get exposed to. Also, pay attention to things that add value to you and contribute to the achievement of your dreams. Having a broad scope is fine at the start, but eventually you should narrow your research and learn deeply rather than broadly; otherwise you will waste time and energy. Go after the right knowledge and get the knack of the necessary things. Determination maintains focus.

Self-Awareness and Determination

Self-awareness is all about knowing your preferences, strengths, and weaknesses, and thus, is about seeing yourself more clearly. If you do not know your own limitations, you will push yourself past reasonable expectation far too quickly and end up feeling unworthy. You need to be able to play to your strengths and foresee potential avenues of development.

No one knows your personality better than you do. But introspection requires practice and genuine care. It is unnerving to realize you can become a stranger to yourself. To prevent this, you have to spend time unraveling your own heart: your motivations, sources of happiness, and deep fears. Once I began committing myself to success, I quickly realized that my methods needed to be about the process, not the product. For me, it really wasn't about the rewards for reaching the next step; it was about falling in love with the progression. And by doing so, I became far more effective. I began treading a path I thought I'd never start, and making moves I had never dared to make.

Again, we must get it straight here: Self-awareness is not *over-awareness*. Self-awareness is not *self-righteousness*. It is *self-cognizance*. If you start second-guessing yourself and questioning every little decision and emotion, you are becoming hyper-fixated. Conversely, if you're refusing to accept insight or observations from those around you, you are becoming self-righteous. Self-awareness is never meant to make you independent of others. It is not there to make you "better than others." It is there to help you build confidence. Even if you are the best in the group—the one whose ideas are the chosen path whenever there is deliberation—you should not parade yourself as such. Be humble enough to take in one or two opinions from others.

It is okay to be the most efficient. It is okay to be the cream of the crop. It is okay to have all that is needed for growth in your circle. But do not become prideful. God opposes the proud but gives grace to the humble (James 4:6). Even Jesus Christ learned from his parents. He was the Son of God, the only begotten Son of the most high. But he learned. He sat and learned.

While you are becoming aware of yourself, pay attention to your weaknesses. It is easier to flaunt your strengths than own up to your weaknesses. There is a compulsion in humans that makes it difficult for them to accept frailty. Being aware of your weak points helps you to focus more on adding fuel to your fire by either addressing those shortcomings personally or surrounding yourself with those who compliment your qualities. It helps you build momentum and muster courage where you need to. It is not enough to identify your weaknesses; seek to overcome them, too. And while you are at it, leverage your strengths.

It takes commitment to your own success to stay on top of every situation. You won't make much progress if you only do hard work when you feel ready. Commitment implies that we stay true to our end goals even when the circumstances are not favorable. Otherwise, we will end up becoming people who shy away from challenges when they arise, even when success is just a stone's throw away.

Unless a commitment is made, there are only empty promises

and hopes, but no plans. It is the repetition that is going to make your end goal stick in your consciousness. If you are ever going to get a way out and create opportunities where there are none, determination is essential.

Actions Speak Louder

You probably already know where I am headed. So, let us journey together. Success is not a passive thing. If it was, we would all be great by now. It costs nothing to make wishes and daydream about success. But what happens next? Are you going to keep talking and talking about your plans without doing anything? Actions speak louder, friend.

Some people will spend all their free time making plans, and at the end of the day, have nothing to show for it. It is necessary to spend quality time analyzing and preparing plans, but that is not the same as making actual moves. Have open discussions and be able to articulate your desires, but don't be afraid to put your money where your mouth is.

There are some who will seem to be on another level because of how determined they sound. They will make you feel lazy. You'll hear them laud, *"I'm never turning back. I hit the mark,"* and *"I will do all I can to achieve my goal. Nothing will stop me. Nothing!"* But the next time you find them, they are still talking. Usually, I say, "Mate, enough talking, get down to business. You do need to actually try." Talk has its place; speaking keeps you conscious of your dream and where you are going. It helps you build confidence in your pursuit and find the strength to keep moving. But it has limits.

When you do more talking than acting, you are really doing nothing! Determination speaks for itself. You would not need to convince the person next to you that you are determined if you really were. It shows in your responses, reactions, and choices. While you should speak up to gain confidence, take practical steps to ensure your words do not come back to you void.

Remember the story Jesus told about the man with two sons? He says in Matthew 21:28-30: *"[The father] went to the older [son] and said, 'Son, go and work in the vineyard today.' 'I don't want to,' he answered, but later he changed his mind and went. Then the father went to the other son and said the same thing. 'Yes, sir,' he answered, but he did not go."*

The lesson here is clear-cut. Just because you say it, even with enthusiasm, it does not mean you will do it. Am I saying it is wrong to make your plans known? No. All I am saying is do not get locked up in the den of words; do not be driven just by words. Act!

Take It Slow

Success is gained in stages. A determined person is not just one who is ecstatic about his dreams, but one who knows how to tread carefully and wait for the right moment. Scattered all over the Scriptures are stories of people who had a clear picture of where they were heading but had to wait patiently: from Father Abraham, who received the promise of a son at age seventy-five but did not bear one until he was one hundred, to King David, who was anointed king in his teens but did not mount the throne until about fifteen years later. There's so much evidence in the Bible that success requires patience, and that only the patient will reap its full benefit.

Between the time when David was anointed by Samuel and when he became king in Israel, he went through painful, irrevocable stages. If bringing down Goliath was not hard enough, then fleeing from Saul certainly troubled his mind. Not only did David have to flee, but he also had to live his life on the run, all so that he could be able to take the throne.

Joseph had a dream that implied he'd have leadership over his household. But he did not gain it immediately. He also had his fair share of turmoil and pain. And it took close to fourteen years after his dream for him to get the position he had been preparing for.

There is nothing as disastrous as diverting all your energy to something that will only bring temporary satisfaction. Success is brought on a step at a time. Determination makes you stand firm when the journey seems eternal. This is not to say you must spend your entire life in one role or at one position. If God did not extend the creation of light to the second day, you should not. Do all that is required for the completion of a stage and move on to the next.

There are lots of misconceptions about success in our world today. Some people believe success only comes for those who can leverage their influence in society, and others think achieving it is just luck. The true principles of success negate thoughts like this, and if you want to go far, you must do away with such false beliefs. You do not have to be a VIP before you can challenge the status quo and make a name for yourself.

Embracing limitations and still reaching for gold are the attributes of a committed, aware mind. Life is not a bed of roses; if we think we can find true happiness quickly, then we don't understand joy. We need to relax while following the process.

Get Out of Denial

In Walter Anderson's words, "Our lives improve only when we take chances—and the first and most difficult risk we can take is to be honest with ourselves." If you are serious about achieving success in life, you have to be honest with yourself. Nothing good comes when you deny reality, act like all is well with you, and pretend there is nothing wrong.

If something is not working, admit it. Then and only then

can you fix it. Your environment is hostile, but you go around defending it? Your relationship is toxic, but you craft excuses for remaining there? Oh no! That is wrong. That will not end well. Forgive the bluntness, but that is the truth. Successful people learn to face their true circumstances and deal with them accordingly.

Denial is not faith. So, do not be deceived; just because you believe in a cause does not mean you should thoughtlessly accept any pain it causes you. And if you would hide under the guise of faith, remember that faith without work is dead. You claim you believe in being positive, and so you disregard all the detriments that are actually happening. You claim you profess what you want and not what you see? Fine. But what are you doing to bring your so-called faith to life? What are you doing to make what you want out of the realm of the unseen and bring it into reality? Nothing? What are you doing to align your professions with your experiences? Nothing still? Then you are missing the point! Ask Abraham, ask David, ask any one of the heroes of faith the Bible talks about in the Book of Hebrews—they would tell you that faith is not a passive thing, that faith is not a blind profession, that faith is not a deception.

Faith gets up early in the morning, chops wood for fire, and puts a saddle on his donkey. Faith takes his son and two of his servants to a mountain in the land of Moriah. And the same faithful man laid his only begotten son on an altar for sacrifice. Faith gets up early in the morning, leaves someone else in charge of his father's sheep, loads supplies, and starts off towards the army camp. Faith runs up to the battle line to ask how his brothers are faring. And faith takes up the challenge to face Goliath.

Change Is Inevitable

The power to change and transform is inherent to man. But somehow, so many of us are scared to embrace change when we finally see it.

Good people often become debilitated by the chatter of their loudest fears. We are all quite capable in our comfort zones, but the moment we start to venture into competitive yet fruitful spaces in our quest for mastery, our fears come up—because we are going out into the unknown. It is human. If we are to consider the psychobiology of it, there is a term called "homeostasis" that suggests that human beings are hardwired for a steady state that keeps them alive. Our bodies are always trying to remain in equilibrium in temperature, energy, nourishment, etc. So, when we come up with a new idea, and we see a new opportunity, we start to leave our comfort zones into the zone of the unknown where greatness lives, and we get scared.

Those who look up to and aspire to be like the true heroes, the true titans, and the true masters should know that those great men and women are not fearless; they've only practiced walking into their fear and living on the razor's edge consistently, to the point where they are comfortable amid their discomfort. That is the great opportunity for you—not to avoid fear, but to be comfortable in the unknown, to be comfortable when you are terrified. And that is what the great artists, the great entrepreneurs, and the great leaders are incredible at doing. So, the first reason good people fail is that their faith is not as strong as their fear. Or, to put it more elegantly: their fears are larger than their faith.

You do not get to build strong faith in a day. We often want to believe in ourselves, but we just cannot find the strength. It takes practice and consistency to increase your faith and make it dominate your fears. Your fears will stop you from pushing forward.

Change always tampers with the status quo and challenges our sense of stability. But here's the catch: change is constant, and so it happens whether you want it or not. We may have our plans mapped out, and our steps carefully prepared, but then life ends up getting in the way. Starting over does not seem feasible, and going back is just as impractical. What do you do? Stop? Well, you may just have to re-strategize and deal with it.

As much as change can appear to be a threat, it can also be an opportunity. Opportunity does not always come with loudspeakers, announcing itself and seeking to be noticed. A determined person sees change as a chance to pause, plan, and push again, even when it does not seem favorable.

Now, let's take this mindset one step further. Imagine you already envisioned a possible negative change right before it happened in real life. It does not come to you as a surprise, and you know just what to do in response. Analyzing our circumstance and thinking ahead helps keep you on guard.

When you are determined to go for success, consider possible roadblocks that may arise in the future and prepare as much as possible for them. Do not get too locked up in your plans and how things are moving along presently. If, for instance, you work from home and you are so used to handling tasks from the comfort of your home—no distraction, no frustration, no discomforts at all—do consider how you would adapt if you had to start commuting to an office. Maybe even mix up your scenery and environment. To be practical, you could get out of your home on some days to work in a library. If you normally wake up at 9 a.m., try getting out of bed earlier. If you take breaks whenever the mood strikes, try sticking to a specific schedule. Playing through these scenarios means that when change must happen, you can take it head-on.

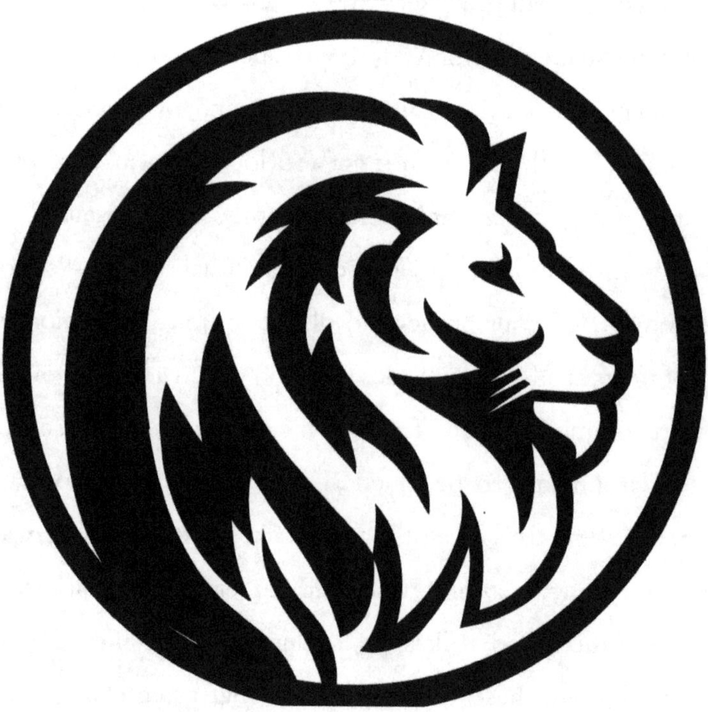

Chapter Six
THE MIRAGE OF PERFECTION

Better is the poor that walketh in his integrity, than he that is perverse in his lips, and is a fool.

—Book of Proverbs

We all have flaws. Like John Stuart Mill said years back, "It is better to be a human being dissatisfied than a pig satisfied; better to be Socrates dissatisfied than a fool satisfied. And if the fool, or the pig, is of a different opinion, it is only because they only know their own side of the question." No man has all that he will ever need within himself. Whether you agree or not, there is a part of you that is yet to be perfected. A perfect person is all-sufficient, just like God, and can never make mistakes. The person I am talking about here is probably still God's future project—he does not exist.

Be Real

You have flaws because you are human. Once you understand that, you should consider doing away with every notion of imperfection being a sin. Those beliefs made you hide your flaws and pretend to be what you are not. And who says that is a step in the right direction? Man is not imperfect because he fails to learn what others knows; man is imperfect because God made us so.

Sadly, men are more unwilling to have their imperfections known than their crimes. But no one on the path to success should be hiding his weaknesses or pretending to be good when, in fact, he is not. Imperfections exist to show what needs to be done. The reason I will go over what I write in every chapter of this book is to be sure I am being honest, direct, and accurate. I am real enough to admit my flaws. I know my work cannot be perfect in the first draft. So, I check again.

Imperfections make you want to get better. You find something lagging today; you push tomorrow to get it in place. You find another imperfection tomorrow; you push on and on until you hit the mark. That is how progress is made. Successful people do not just maintain what they are able to achieve today. If they did, Apple's net income would not have grown from $1.3 trillion in 2019 to $2 trillion in 2020. They realized there was room for more, and a lot could still be achieved, so they kept pushing.

Be real. There's no harm in saying, *"I haven't gotten this right. I need to learn."* The harm is in trying to deceive others and prove that you're the best. If you succeed in deceiving everyone around you today, you might not tomorrow. As a matter of fact, you would only end up deceiving yourself.

Imperfections can be fixed. And that is the goal. It is not enough to identify your flaws; you must be intentional about getting better.

Finding the Balance

There is a duality to man in how we strive to become the best we can despite the fact that we can never be flawless. Perfection may be an impossibility, but you can become whoever you want to be; you might not be the ideal, but you'll be near enough to have that satisfaction. Recall Jesus said to His disciples, *"Be ye therefore perfect, even as your Father which is in heaven is perfect,"* and He strived to be as close to an ideal man as He could (Matthew 5:48).

The fact that you are imperfect is not an excuse to be unproductive. While you admit your imperfections and confess your flaws, take practical steps to make sure you improve. You have to be the one to push yourself; you alone can know just how far you can reach. If you decide to blame others and live in the past, you might never move forward.

God made us with imperfections. Yes. But He never intended

for this to paralyze us. We are made in His image. He sent His only Son to the world to live as man. God made us imperfect so we could go after what makes for perfection.

But do not let your imperfections be your downfall. You don't have to think too far; Lucifer is a good example.

You should always strive to be more; there is a problem when you no longer see a need to. But self-improvement is not something you achieve by being covetous or overly ambitious. It is step-by-step attainment. Take time to build up your weaknesses and be sure they do not ruin you.

Courage

The concept of courage has, over time, been subject to a lot of misconceptions and false beliefs. Of course, it takes courage to be heroic like Samson. But is being courageous all about being a hero in a physical sense? I do not think so. It is easier to call Samson a hero for putting his life on the line than to consider David one. And that is a problem.

This is what I mean: King David was vulnerable; each time he wrote, he made his imperfections known. That is the height of heroism for me. Anybody can be seen as brave when they are showcasing power and fighting a just cause, but who dares sacrifice his reputation on the altar of valor? We need heroes in our society today. And what can be more heroic than speaking openly and honestly about who we are? What can be more heroic than putting your status aside so that the world may know of your flaws? Nothing!

The reason most of us do not see courage every day is that we lack courage ourselves. It takes courage to own up to imperfections. And like Brené Brown wrote in her book *The Gifts of Imperfection,* "Every time we choose courage, we make everyone around us a little better and the world a little braver." Imagine there are a few students in a classroom who are completely lost in a lesson, and each one decides to keep mum for fear of being scorned or seen as unintelligent. The moment one of them decides to raise their hand in front of their forty other classmates and ask for help is the day the others gain freedom too. The problem is, everyone cares more about what others think of them than what their lot is at the end of the day. And if I would be honest, the fault is not always theirs. In the past, some may have been bullied, or teachers may have been exasperated at their confusion.

There was a time I received an invitation to speak to a group of young adults on this subject. I spoke and spoke for hours, like a church pastor aiming to invigorate his chapel, and just as I was about to round off the discussion, someone hissed. The sound was so shocking that I had to convince myself that it was not a snake. *What exactly is going on? Why would someone hiss like that? Does it mean I have been spewing lies for the past two hours?* Oh my! I could not get those questions out of my head as I finished up.

"Thanks for having me, guys. I'm honored," I concluded. Then I managed to add, "And if you're not comfortable with anything I said, let us talk." Even though I wasn't sure what I would say if someone, especially a young mind, confronted me, I was intent on knowing why someone would hiss that loud.

I sat there at the back of the auditorium, hoping to meet with my adversary and maybe apologize for being so hate-worthy to deserve such an animalistic noise. And in just a couple of minutes, he came. I smiled, and it was probably obvious that my grin was forced. The young man smiled back, and that was enough relief for me.

Long story short, we talked. And after the conversation, I understood everything. He told me about how his imperfections had been used against him because he'd opened up. He wasn't too good at working under pressure, and he preferred having ample time to deal with tasks. He'd told his "friends" about this, and they'd used it against him. They'd told his would-be employer that this prospective employee would be a bad fit for the company because he was "too slow" and could not work under pressure. And that was the end. How cruel!

Through our conversation, I learned an entirely new perspective—that it is better to keep your flaws close to your chest when you do not have the right people around. I learned that not everyone who keeps mum about their shortcomings is being pretentious; some are trying to stay safe.

So, at times, people pretend. And then they dread coming out and saying things just the way they are. The responses of our peers will shape how we act on our flaws. Some friends will hear your tales of error and respond with covering praise, acting like you are "too good" to make such mistakes. Other friends respond with even greater concern and distress than you did. And then there are some who disregard any problems you confess to, never minding if you repeat the same mistakes. They hide under the guise of *"We're all human"* to make you see no need for improvement.

But are we going to keep hiding flaws because friends are flawed themselves? God forbid!

What shall we say, then? If your friends fall under any of these categories I have mentioned, or if they are even worse, you need to address their behaviors directly. And if they continue on, you may not need them. You need friends who would empathize with you rather than shower you with unnecessary sympathy.

In Brené Brown's words, "…[W]e need someone who is deeply rooted, able to bend, and, most of all, we need someone who embraces us for our strengths and struggles. We need to honor our struggle by sharing it with someone who has earned the right to hear it. When we're looking for compassion, it's about connecting with the right person at the right time about the right issue."

Do not lose your courage because someone has failed to be a responsible friend. While you work to make today's flaws tomorrow's strength, while you work to break out of your limitations and soar like an eagle in the air, remember the law of process: *"For precept must be upon precept, precept upon precept; line upon line, line upon line; here a little, and there a little"* (Isaiah 28:10).

The Gift of Imperfection

You should never get tired of hearing this line: *imperfection is a gift*. If I decide to repeat the same throughout this chapter and the next, you should love it. There are so many beautiful things about being imperfect; you probably haven't noticed because you saw the whole thing as a curse.

The rewards of imperfection are not for the faint of heart. You cannot remain in your past, wallowing in what you could have done better, and also receive these gifts I am talking about here. They are for those who are humble enough to be open and brave enough to move on.

To be honest, this is not an easy thing to do. You need to be able to address your past clinically and determines what lessons have been imparted to you. According to Brené Brown, "We don't change, we don't grow, and we don't move forward without the work [of being vulnerable]. If we really want to live a joyful, connected, and meaningful life, we must talk about things that get in the way."

Success is one of the greatest gifts of imperfection, although this may seem contradictory. When we learn to reach out during our struggles and be honest, we can connect with those who have once been in our shoes and be graced with their wisdom. That alone is comfort. You'll know you are not abnormal for making mistakes, and that there is someone who understands what it means to have flaws.

I must add here that, while you seek out those you trust to share your struggles with, you should aim to be that person for others. Be that person who does not shy away from his weaknesses and empathizes with his friends. Be that person who can understand when someone is not getting it right and admit that he was once there. Be that person who knows just what to say when someone is caught in the web of imperfections. *"Do to others what you would have them do to you"* (Matthew 7:12).

Exercising Faith

Faith means different things to different people—to some, it is the act of believing before seeing; to others, it is the substance of things hoped for (Hebrews 11:1). Whatever your definition, faith is an essential part of living, and a life without faith is not a life worth living. You know, there is no real freedom without the knowledge of what is true.

Faith is the evidence of things not seen, according to the Bible (Hebrews 11:1). And what this means is: though I have not gotten it, I will act as if I have. Faith is active, a substance, evidence.

What am I talking about? Here's a quote from Hebrews 11:7 and 11:27-30:

> Because Noah had faith, he was warned about something that had not yet happened. He obeyed and built a boat that saved him and his family. [...] Because of his faith, Moses left Egypt. Moses had seen the invisible God and wasn't afraid of the king's anger. [...] Because of their faith, the people walked through the Red Sea on dry land. But when the Egyptians tried to do it, they were drowned. God's people had faith, and when they had walked around the city of Jericho for seven days, its walls fell down.

Faith has never been anything passive. So, while you want to have faith and believe you will lay hold of your desired success, remember also to act.

Now, what has faith got to do with imperfections? Faith is what makes you try again after failing. Deep down, you are sure of something; you know there is a successful end that only comes true when you forge ahead. Without faith, it is impossible to get better. How do you explain to a faithless computer programmer who has gotten used to trying and failing that he can be just as good as Bill Gates? How do you convince a writer who sees nothing good in his content to keep churning out stories? There's probably no way. Once you no longer believe that you can attain the peak of your potential, you will stop making headway. All that will probably matter to you is focusing on what you know you can do well. You will be a local champion, so long as you don't have to try something that "doesn't work."

Successful people love to explore. They love to check out other possibilities. And that is how they grow. Growth is moving gradually from where you are to where you ought to be. You do not grow by lying cool in your comfort zone, and you cannot grow without faith. Faith recognizes today's flaws but believes more in tomorrow's perfection. Faith admits today's Jericho but walks 'round and 'round it till it is completely brought down.

The Dark Side of Perfectionism

Perfectionism sounds like great stuff. I mean, who wouldn't want to have a burning desire to ensure everything is exactly how it ought to be? It is easy to see a goal in this and pursue it vigorously. But is perfectionism always great? Is it something you should think of making your life mission? I do not think so.

A lot of research has shown that the quest for perfection has, in fact, more flaws than it does benefits. A Forbes article written by Jules Schroeder says, "*On one hand, [perfectionism] holds you to high standards and ensures you only create exceptional work. But on the other hand, those same standards bind you, causing you to procrastinate, avoid action, and be less effective.*"

Perfectionism will paralyze you at the mere idea of making an error. You believe you are the "best," so you only act when success feels guaranteed. If you are going to achieve great success, you must be willing to grab the bull by its horns; and you must dare to explore new grounds and make mistakes if necessary. Do not shut people off because they are not doing things your way. Who says your way is always the ideal way? Who says there are no better ways of getting things done?

Perfectionism keeps you in a box and gives you a false definition of right and wrong. It makes everything seem like nothing to you; your accomplishments only matter if they are pristine. And that sucks. No matter how little, an achievement is an achievement. Being a perfectionist makes you see little wins as no wins, and nothing you achieve feels good enough. Some will think you are only proud about loud things—the things that make people notice you and praise you for the rest of their lives. Successful people do not act like that. They try everything they can, whether it is likely to succeed or not. They celebrate little wins even as they get set for bigger ones.

If you are an "all or nothing" thinker, then you are a perfectionist. It is good to aim high, of course; high achievers do so. But perfectionists are different. They aim high, and if they don't reach their goals, it's soul-crushing. When there is a little error or glitch, they divert attention to it and act like the entire project failed.

Perfectionism does not make you perfect. It only makes you worse. Instead of beating yourself up over minor flaws and seeking to be the "no mistake" kind of person, practice vulnerability.

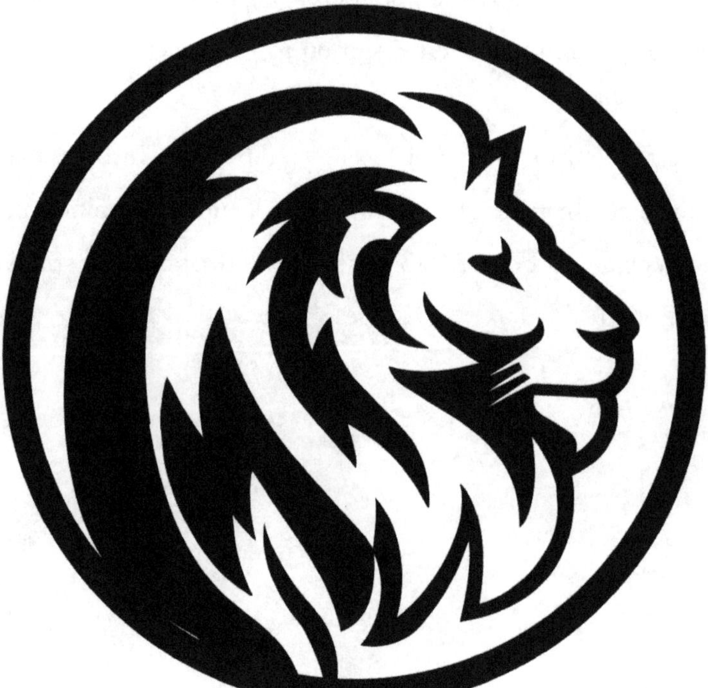

Chapter Seven
MISTAKES & FAILURES

For though the righeous fall seven times, they rise again.
—Book of Proverbs

It is important to understand that learning from your mistakes does not happen automatically—it requires thinking and reflection.

Acknowledge

Our inherently egoistic, self-justifying nature prevents us from seeing ourselves honestly. This inherent nature does not permit us to find the root of all our problems within ourselves, so we are always quick to blame others or external circumstances. But once you can manage this instinct and prioritize introspection, you can make progress on yourself far more quickly.

Mistakes are part of our daily lives. George Bernard Shaw said, "A life spent making mistakes is not only more honorable, but more useful than a life spent doing nothing." And this is largely true. Why? Oprah Winfrey told me to tell you, dear reader, to "Think like a queen. A queen is not afraid to fail. Failure is another steppingstone to greatness." Making mistakes proves that you are trying, growing, learning. Do not think of your mistakes as marks against your character or evidence of your inability. Think of them as trial and error.

Those in a position of leadership who shame others for making mistakes are massively detrimental, and this behavior undercuts their team's performance. Being shamed for trying will result in a timid nature; you are taught that your attempts aren't appreciated, you become afraid to try, you miss opportunities, and you are unable to be creative. As we discussed before, perfectionism is a curse, and those who refuse to act unless they know they will be entirely correct are severely limited.

Ask

Your mistakes have happened, and so be it. But that is not the end. Learn from your errors by asking questions. "Why did I make that brash decision? Was I upset, in a rush?" or "How did I not see that fallout coming? What warning signs did I ignore?"

Once you can discern your motive and discover why you

made the mistake, you can move on to:

"What can I learn from this?" and "How do I avoid this in the future?" or even "What could I have done to mitigate the effects of my mistake?" These questions help you understand how to avoid repeated errors and what your personal trouble areas are.

Steve Jobs said, "Sometimes when you innovate, you make mistakes. It is best to admit them quickly, and get on with improving your other innovations." I never really grasped that quote until I read that he got fired from Apple—the company he created—in 1985. Like, what??

Well, that allowed him to reassess and start from scratch with new projects such as NeXT and Pixar. Eventually, he re-entered Apple and became CEO, showing that passion can be stronger than failure.

While you're admitting to your mistake, but not beating yourself up for it, ask those tough and important questions. This helps you gradually heal from the pain of the error.

Like the writers in my circle always say, "Writing is a great form of healing; it exposes the joy, pain, and hurt a person feels in lines." Reader, it is important to write down your questions and your responses, so you will see the situation a little more clearly. Seeing every element on paper, and thus removed from you, can help you think more logically about an irrational or emotional experience. Keeping a journal is also a great idea.

Don't be afraid to laugh at yourself while you're answering these questions. A little humor goes a long way.

Crafting A Plan

Many people tend to gloss over their errors, and therefore they inevitably fail to learn from them.

You must first recognize that an occurrence was a mistake; if not, you'll repeat that error and it will snowball into a terrible habit.

When a mistake becomes a habit, it is much harder to break. For example, a mistake is forgetting to lock your shop door. A habit is continually choosing not to lock the door so you can get in faster during the morning. There's no harm done until you enter one morning to see that your inventory has been stolen, or your walls vandalized.

From drinking too heavily to gambling too much, you'll start to recognize this pattern in those whose lives are slowly spiraling. To break out of these bad habits, you'll need the discipline that we discussed before. My advice? Make a plan that will help you avoid making a similar mistake. Be as detailed as possible but remain flexible since your plan may need to change. For example, having a firm schedule in the morning so that you arrive at work with time to spare will limit the desire to leave the door unlocked. Likewise, you can cut back your alcohol one drink at a time, or even quit cold turkey and remove yourself from tempting situations altogether.

Find an accountability partner or track your progress on a calendar; just find a way to hold yourself accountable. When you make a mistake, do not feel that you must cope with it on your own. Talk to your mates or family about it. They might provide some perspective that sheds light on what happened and makes you feel a little better. Keep in mind that what works for one person might not work for someone else.

A Hard Way

With this section, I hope to prepare you for the fact that the goals you aim to achieve will most likely involve hard choices and resolutions. Above all else, you need to believe in yourself. Your methods won't always be perfect, but you need to try, and once you find a plan that works, keep at it. I know there's a part of you asking the "What if?" questions, but do not let doubt cloud your vision. Creating a list of all the reasons why you should stay on track can help you remain disciplined, even during the toughest times. Quit focusing on the failures and focus on what and who you are fighting for.

One hard way is forgiveness. Not only for others, but for yourself. Yes, it is hard—especially when the result of your mistake is awful, or when it has hurt those you care about—

but you must forgive yourself. The truest but most difficult form of healing is forgiveness. If you can learn to forgive yourself, you will find yourself more caring and kind to the world at large, and hardier against others' cruel condemnations.

And just in case you fall off the horse, get up again, pick up the plan, and stick to it. Remember, if most inventions and methods are improved through trial and error: not erring would mean rarely improving.

Your Last Mistake Is Your Best Teacher

Naturally, in the journey to success, you need to devote yourself to correcting mistakes and growing from them. However, if this eats up too much of your mental space, you will become hyperaware of your flaws. There is a very thin line between learning from mistakes and becoming overly conscious of them. When you have your mind fixed on mistakes, chances are you will continue to make them. You can't have your consciousness fixated on what you want to avoid; it's a paradox. Life is a risk. When I decide to spread my wings and try something new for the very first time, I am bearing a risk—it may or may not flop. But I will not approach it with a failure mindset. I will not expect to fail just because it is my first time. I will simply give it my best shot and watch what happens next.

I know a man who gets bothered whenever he tries something

for the first time and succeeds without committing blunders. You don't believe it? Oh, I didn't either; it sounds too strange to be real. But trust me, I met this man. He had a reason for thinking this way, and it came from the loads of "motivational" lectures he had received in the past. He had been informed that success achieved without mistakes is no real success. Whoever said that must be the worst "advisor" on Earth. How exactly do you prove this—that every success MUST flow from some record of failures or mistakes? (If you have ever had such a notion, now is a good time to trash it in the bin and leave it there for keeps). No hard feelings, but that is an extreme line of thought.

Do humans make mistakes? Yes. Will humans make mistakes? Yes. Must humans make mistakes? No. All I am trying to say here is that you should avoid being *mistake-conscious*. Mistake-consciousness instills fear that will cause you to commit blunders. It's a self-fulfilling prophecy. You can try this: Pick up a glass of water and occupy your mind with possible mistakes you can make while moving around your room with the glass in your hand. Then move, still thinking of the mistakes. It is only a matter of time before you hit your leg against a chair and spill the water over. The point is: expecting to make mistakes will ensure you make mistakes; it does not save you from them.

The last mistake you made is your best teacher for the next step you would take. Recall I talked about the law of process—

line upon line, here a little, and there a little (Isaiah 28:10). Every stage has its lessons.

The mistake I most strongly advise against is one that you have already committed in the past. This will happen at some point, when you are convinced you can change outcomes or when the retribution didn't sting all that much. But repeating mistakes shows that you haven't learned from your experience. There is no harm in changing your strategy or approach if the path you are treading does not seem like the way to go. Yes, it is great to stay your course and push hard, but do not get stuck there. While you want to be determined, watch out for all future possibilities. Not everyone is a Thomas Edison—you might not need to fail 999 times before recording success. So, if there are other, better ways to make it work, try them out.

Two Sides of the Coin: Mistakes and Failures

After taking a personal survey of the perceptions and beliefs of those around me, I realized most people confuse mistakes with failures these days. In Seth Godin's words, "A failure is a project that doesn't work, an initiative that teaches you something at the same time the outcome doesn't move you directly closer to your goal. A mistake is either a failure repeated, doing something for the second time when you should have known better, or a misguided attempt […] that hindsight reminds you is worth avoiding."

Failures often happen when we try something new, but they are not always the results of mistakes made. When a person embarks on a project for the first time, he is unsure what works and what does not. He is only going to do his best and give the project his utmost. And even though his efforts determine, to a reasonable extent, the project's outcome, they are not an automatic guarantee of success. Experience often drives the success of a project; if you have done something over and over again, you have probably become a pro at it. This is more or less similar to the 10,000-hour rule popularized by Malcolm Gladwell. Simply put, the key to expertise is long hours of persistent practice.

On the other hand, mistakes happen when we take actions or make decisions that are unwise. They could be a result of carelessness, ignorance, or various misconceptions. Still, they do not always lead to failures.

Failures can either result from making the same mistakes repeatedly or taking drastic steps without proper planning. If you are used to doing things without caution, chances are high you would do that which will cost you success someday. One has failed when they've made a drastic enough error that they cannot move forward, or when misfortune falls upon others and not just themselves.

Learn, Unlearn, and Learn Again

In this chapter, I said that learning from mistakes does not happen automatically. Lessons do not jump at you because you have made a mistake. Therefore, people make the same mistakes repeatedly. At the end of every mistake is (or ought to be) learning. I try this; it fails. I try it again; it fails. Then, I learn.

It takes discipline and determination to glean meaning from our mistakes. You need first to admit you are wrong—tell yourself the truth and try to be honest. The goal is not to feel bad or give up on doing things right; it is to draw lessons and move on with better perceptions. As John writes in the first chapter of his first Epistle, *"If we claim to be without sin, we deceive ourselves and the truth is not in us. If we confess our sins, [H]e is faithful and just and will forgive us our sins and purify us from all unrighteousness. If we claim we have not sinned, we make [H]im out to be a liar and [H]is word is not in us"* (I John 1:8-10). It is only through acknowledging, accepting, and addressing your shortcomings that you can ever hope to move forward and progress as a person, friend, teammate, and leader.

IT TAKES COMMITMENT TO YOUR OWN SUCCESS TO STAY ON TOP OF EVERY SITUATION. YOU WON'T MAKE MUCH PROGRESS IF YOU ONLY DO HARD WORK WHEN YOU FEEL READY.

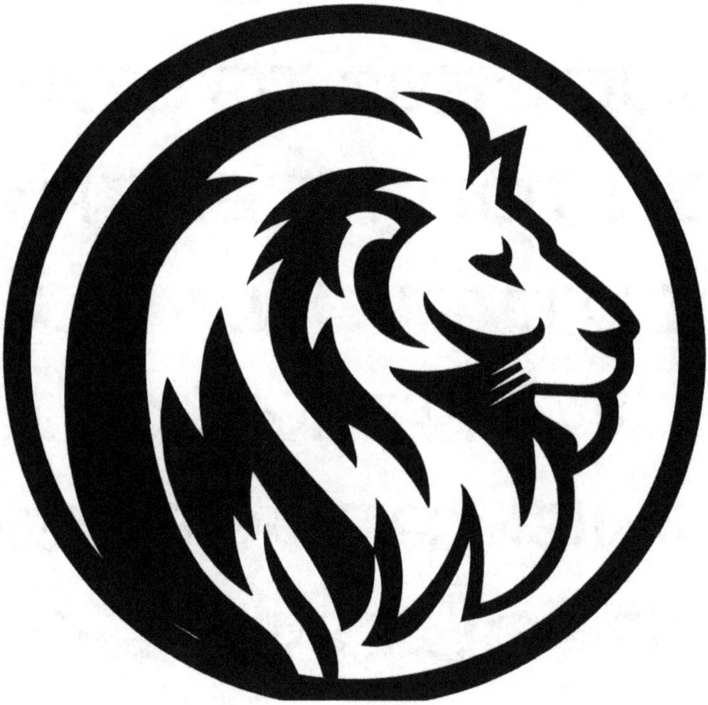

Chapter Eight
TIMING

In their hearts humans plan their course, but the Lord establishes their steps.
—Book of Proverbs

Time is so often the enemy. We are racing against the clock, trying to finish so many tasks in a day or so many assignments in a semester. Successful people understand that when to act is just as important as how. "No matter how well prepared you are, how great the idea is, or how keen your team, if the timing isn't right, you're battling uphill from the start. Thankfully, there are lines of inquiry that can help to gauge the likelihood of whether you're about to push straight out of the bay onto rough seas," stated Design Thinking-company Pascal Satori while discussing the findings of Bill Gross, founder of Idealab.

The law of timing has its root in the Bible. It states that *"There is a time for everything, and a season for every activity under the heavens: a time to be born and a time to die, a time to plant and a time to uproot, a time to kill and a time to heal, a time to tear down and a time to build, a time to weep and a time to laugh, a time to mourn and a time to dance, a time to scatter stones and a time to gather them, a time to embrace and a time to refrain from embracing, a time to search and a time to give up…"* (Ecclesiastes 3:1-6). This simply points to the fact that not every positive action is right at every moment. When you have decided which turn to take, another important consideration is when to make it. There is a need to take each step at the right time; it is necessary if you would reap the full fruit of your labor.

Why Timing Goes Wrong

The most common reasons for bad timing are pressure and ignorance.

Pressure from peers or society can force you into acting too quickly or make you miss your opportunity. We see our friends and acquaintances succeed and think, *"I can do that too."* And so, we jump into something entirely new, expecting to receive the exact same results as someone who started months before.

But we are not all the same. Someone else's success does not guarantee yours. Yes, the pressure could be capable of pushing you beyond your limits, but the ball is in your court—

you determine where and how it is played. Do not give in to pressure to do things you are not prepared for. Take your time and learn the ropes. Your time will come, and when it does, you will do more without hassle or struggle. The best way to learn from someone else's success is to get close and learn from their mistakes. Too often, we become so fascinated by achievement that we forget to consider failure.

Conversely, we may be influenced by others that we are being too brash, too bold. This is why it is vital to trust your instincts. You must have the confidence to strike when the iron is hot, to get ahead of the curve and be a groundbreaker when necessary. Wrong timing can hamper all you have been building for years and prevent your dreams from becoming a reality.

The other common reason for wrong timing is ignorance. Before setting out at all, find out everything you need to know about the steps you will be taking. Ask questions like, *"What comes first?", "When is the time to strike?", "At what point do I lay cool?",* and *"What do I do after this?"* They will help you get familiar with the right timing, so you won't be acting solely on impulse. A man who acts without planning is like one who goes on a trip without his luggage.

Every step matters on the long road to victory. You need to pay attention to the details and commit yourself fully to bring your dreams to reality.

Your Mentality of Timing

In Ecclesiastes 8:6, the Bible says there is a right time and a right way to do everything. But we know so little! This can be painfully transparent for those who are misguided in their perception of timing.

Some mistakenly believe there is no such thing as "the wrong time for the right action." This is incorrect on a basic sense—you don't decide to sleep during your work shift—but also in the success-driven sense that you have to accept your goals are going to take consistent effort, and therefore you have to be strategic and thoughtful. For example, if you have a major exam or presentation and want to do well, you don't start preparing the night before. This would be the right action at the wrong time. Instead, you have to think ahead and give yourself the opportunity to make the correct decisions where they're necessary instead of panicking as the pressure builds.

Time is not an overwhelming, unstoppable force that you're constantly battling against. You can learn how to make time work for you, and how to accept it as a part of nature that is delivering you to your ultimate resolution of achievement.

Be Patient

I consider patience a virtue that is gradually becoming extinct. In today's world, everyone wants to get the best out of life in the shortest time possible. I believe it's a consequence of so much of our lives being digital. While technology has given us marvelous advancements and opportunity for happiness and knowledge, there are plenty of downsides. On social media, people only promote their best sides, and this makes us envious, and our comparisons dishonest. We're craving to mirror lives that aren't being accurately represented. And with the immediacy of technology—automatic shopping and home delivery, live-update news, and immediate responses—we are overloaded with instant gratification.

But personal success, in your career and as a person, does not work like that. It takes patience to stay the course and take steps when they are necessary. *"Do it now," "Carpe diem," "Go for it,"* and other instant-action triggers we get from motivational speakers are the reason some of us will never get things right. No, the harm is not in the words themselves; it is in their effect. You want to do it now, but you do not know how it is done. You want to get it now, but you do not even know how to handle it. You want to go for it, but you do not even know what is next. Am I suggesting you stay idle and groundless? No. The point is clear: whatever your desires, whatever your dreams, whatever your goals and aspirations, learn to lay low and take things slowly.

Being Time-Conscious

You know, I could have stayed glued to my PC until I finished this book in one go, but I am human, not a robot. I take breaks, and I rest.

Not everyone has schedules that favor the rule of peak periods, but we can find ways to put our energy dips in check. One reliable way is taking successive breaks. *"Work smarter, not harder"* includes adapting to your energy and attention levels and adapting your work so that you're most efficient.

If you have got too much on your hands and you have little time to provide results, you will probably want to concentrate your efforts on getting everything done within the short time available. But after spending a couple of hours working, you will realize you are getting drained, and your energy is gradually running out. It happens to me. I want to write as many words as possible, but after writing a paragraph, my strength fails. What? I have not even churned out five hundred words yet, and this is happening? At such times, I am left with just one option—take a break.

One way to have a better grasp of time management is to try different methods or styles. The Pomodoro Technique developed by Francesco Cirillo is excellent for large projects or studying; it breaks work sessions into intervals, typically twenty-five minutes with five-minute breaks.

Whether you are a nocturnal or diurnal person, taking short time-outs is important. Being a night owl is not enough reason to be ineffective during the day and being a morning person does not stop you from being productive at night. There are times you must go against your norm; you do not tell your boss you are a night owl when he asks you to work on a task by day.

Proper timing will teach you when to work and when to halt. You will have no problem doing the right things at the right time if you take regular breaks.

One good way to learn proper timing is to be conscious of time. I used to have friends who never had regard for time management. Fix a meeting with them for 10 a.m., and you would be sure to wait some two hours more. No, they were not bad people; they had only formed a habit of tardiness. I had to limit the scope of our friendship as their lackluster commitment to time started to rub off on me. These little things—punctuality and time-consciousness—matter, because they are the small steps upon which greatness is built.

In the study titled "Time, Consciousness, and Mind Uploading" by Yoonsuck Choe, Jaerock Kwon, and Ji Ryang Chung, it was suggested that, "The function of the brain is intricately woven into the fabric of time. Functions such as (i) storing and accessing *past* memories, (ii) dealing with immediate sensorimotor needs in the *present*, and (iii) projecting into the *future* for goal-directed behavior are good examples of how key brain processes are integrated into time." They went further to state that "Moreover, it can even seem that the brain *generates* time (in the psychological sense, not in the physical sense) since, without the brain, a living organism cannot have the notion of past nor future."

Time-consciousness is not merely being aware of the time; it's understanding both how time and its perceived pressures affect you, and how you respond to them. The experience of time is subjective, not only for events and memories, but in how you view deadlines, dates, and future plans.

To make the most of your time, you need to be in control of yourself.

Chapter Nine
CLOSED DOORS

Because you know that the testing of your faith produces perseverance.
—**Book of James**

And we know that in all things God works for the good of those who love him, who have been called according to his purpose.
—**Book of Romans**

Opportunities come but once, they say, but what do you do when opportunities do not come? Relax? Mourn? Or...hope? Well, it is up to you.

Many of us grew up with the belief that life is designed to bring us good tidings automatically—that we do not have to push hard, we only need to "believe," and then success will come knocking at our doors. While this is no lie at all (faith makes all things possible), this passive understanding of success can do much more harm than we could have ever imagined.

Yes, you need to have faith in God and believe in your dreams. But some opportunities do not come readily; they wait to be sought after. There are times you must create opportunities for yourself; they do not exist yet, but they can be brought into existence.

I love to draw life lessons from the maker of life Himself—God. The Bible describes the state of the Earth before creation as "void" and "without form" (Genesis 1:2). From that, it is safe to assume there was no opportunity for *making* at all—no favorable circumstance to aid creation in whatever way. But something happened. God spoke: *"Let there be,"* and there was. He could have chosen not to speak. He could have kept roaming and roaming without doing a thing. But no, He did not. God created simply by speaking. That is exactly what I am talking about here. If you do not act, it's possible nothing may happen.

God Is the Doorkeeper

Let us talk about how closed doors—hindrances and barriers on the path to success—cannot stop you. We've all had hard times when our hopes didn't work out, or even when nothing was going right in our lives—when we did not get a promotion, the loan did not go through, a relationship did not make it. We did our best, prayed, believed, but the door still did not open. We are pushed to the wall, and we just cannot be pushed any further. But is that going to be the end of it all? No.

I once talked to a young man that was hoping to get into medical school. He had finished his undergraduate studies and done very well. He had applied to forty different colleges, but none of them had said yes. He got so discouraged, thinking it was not meant to be. But, God would not have allowed the door to close if it were going to keep Him from fulfilling His purpose. Sometimes, doors close to give room for better entrances. Some opportunities do not come because we deserve better ones. This may sound so unrealistic, but it is the truth. There were times I got rejections back to back, and it felt as though the attention of Hell was directly on me. But shortly after, I had much better offers.

We may not see how it will work out, but God never runs out of options. He is never at a loss at how to turn your situation around and make all doors fly open. Little wonder the Bible says God opens doors no man can shut, and he shuts doors no man can open (Revelation 3:7). God is your doorkeeper. In all your ways, acknowledge Him and be sure He will lead you down the right path.

Again, we need to strike a balance. God shuts and opens doors at will and makes all things work together for good. But God is no magician. God is not a basis for sheer irresponsibility.

God will not do what you ought to do for yourself. While you want to hope that God will open doors of opportunity and make all things beautiful, be willing to take action for your dreams.

God is the doorkeeper, but we have got the keys. God does not need the keys to close the doors or keep them open; we do. So, God handed us the keys, as a father to a child. Some of us take the keys and are careless with them, and then when we need them, we go to God crying, *"Father, the doors are closed, and the keys are lost."* Others of us will learn, eventually, the great weight of such freedom. God keeps the door, but we have responsibility as well.

When Doors Close

What do you do when opportunities are nowhere within your reach? What happens when doors close right before your eyes? We all have different perspectives on life, and this determines our responses at such times. Some people are quick to resign to fate and accept whatever comes as "God's will," while others would go to any length to make things work out as planned. But here is the truth: closed doors do not always have to be related to the spiritual. Sometimes, they are just our fault. We could have missed an important step. We could have made the wrong choice. We could have failed in one respect or another. When doors close, find a way out.

It is easy to break down in defeat or get discouraged when opportunities cease. You might even transfer blame and hang your "misfortune" on someone else. But that is not a way forward. If, for instance, you are working on a project and, due to limited resources, you are unable to make headway, you might want to scale down a little bit and work with what you have. While limited resources could be a closed door in this case, resource management could be a way out.

Yes, there are other crucial, more delicate instances of closed doors—for example, financial constraints or limited advancement opportunities. Still, if you do not learn to manage little drags, bigger ones might get overwhelming.

How to Open Closed Doors

Closed doors can be opened. But there is a process, a skill to it. You do not push them open with brute force because they'd break. You can't force an opportunity you are not entitled to; you might lose other opportunities in the process. I will show you how to open closed doors, and keep in mind that these are not the regular "tips and tricks" you would find on the internet; these are real-life principles.

Knock, and Keep Knocking!

Persistence can get you to places you would have never

thought possible. Let's say you are home one day, and someone comes knocking on the door. And you say, "I don't want to be bothered today. I need some time to myself. Okay?"

But the person keeps knocking, making you lose your mind, and you say, "What is it? Who on God's green Earth are you? What do you want? Can you go away?" But the knock never stops. You are left with no other option than to get up and open the door.

This is the same thing Jesus Christ discussed in Luke 18:2-5: *"In a certain city there was a judge who neither feared God nor respected man. And there was a widow in that city who kept coming to him and saying 'Give me justice against my adversary.' For a while he refused, but afterward he said to himself, 'Though I neither fear God nor respect man, yet because this widow keeps bothering me, I will give her justice, so that she will not beat me down by her continual coming.'"*

Have persistence. Closed doors will open if you can endure, so knock and keep knocking. I understand how it feels to be ignored, calling and calling but getting no answer, and I also understand being disturbed when you'd rather have quiet. If it takes "disturbing" the door to get it to open, then go ahead. Do not give up. That you have tried once, twice, or even thrice is not enough reason to back out. Some doors are stubborn, but all they need is for you to keep knocking.

Learn the Ropes

When you want access to a new place, you need to start at the ground level. This means: do your research. Get familiar with the fundamentals, whether that's the core abilities of a new hobby or the background of an industry. Learn who the pros are, who's up-and-coming, and what's been revolutionary in the realm. If you want to get in, you have to talk the talk—you don't want to seem utterly ignorant, or arrogant about your abilities. Often, a little humility and appreciation of what came before you are needed. Sometimes, getting the door to open is all about learning the right way to knock.

Pray and Trust God!

"Trust in the Lord with all your heart. Never rely on what you think you know. Remember the Lord in everything you do, and he will show you the right way. Never let yourself think that you are wiser than you are; simply obey the Lord and refuse to do wrong" (Proverbs 3:5-7).

While self-reliance is an admirable trait, do not forget there is a God up there. Prayer works, and it makes things happen. When doors are closed upon you and nothing seems to be going right, pray. Prayer is simply a communication between you and the Supreme Being. It is an acknowledgment of your imperfections and God's majesty. You pray because you are not perfect. Face it; there is a limit to what you can do for yourself.

So, instead of relying solely on your efforts and human wisdom, trust God to make a way for you. You may be hardworking or highly innovative, but if God does not crown your efforts, they are worth nothing. You are not completely self-sufficient, and you can never be. Trust God.

Alternative Routes

From my experience of unexpected twists and disappointing endings, the old adage holds true: when one door closes, another opens. Not every block in the road is a bad thing; not every detour means you are off track. They could just be a means to a better end—an opportunity to break new ground. Have faith that even when you cannot see the road ahead, you are still moving in the right direction. You probably do not know what to do, where to go, or how to move, but do not fret; trust the process and believe you are exactly where you need to be right now.

What you are going through is what is best for your dream. There is a price to pay for every prize. I am not a preacher of doom, but hard times will surely come. The fact that you are not finding a way out does not mean there is no other route there. It reminds me of the story of the Israelites after their exit from the pangs of Pharaoh. The Red Sea was a hindrance, one that prevented them from reaching the Promised Land. But right in the middle of the sea was a path to tread. Call it the Red Sea, but I would regard it as a closed door.

Success requires growth, and growth is, in fact, not comfortable. I still remember growth spurts, and how much my knees would hurt because I was growing so fast. Growth is uncomfortable, so things are likely to get more and more uncomfortable until you are left with no other choice than to make a change. Change could be anything—taking an entirely different route, digging new wells in your field, anything at all. Trust your intuition, trust God, and trust the process. If you could look at your life from the perspective of your future self, you would see that everything you have been through until now was exactly how it was supposed to be.

In a way, you are the architect of your own life—you have free will, and your intuition leads you through all the things you need to grow. Life is not happening *to* you; it is happening *for* you. When doors close, look around, and find other paths that lead to the same end you desire. You cannot see closed doors as the end of the road. You have to move on, so you can find another route.

Deal with Every Disappointment

Sometimes in life, we give all our willpower and effort, but we do not get any results. And then we tend to get disappointed. But remember this: every disappointment is an event with no meaning in itself; we decide what meaning to attach to it.

We are naturally prone to giving up quickly. The first time we get turned away, we go home. The first time we try the diet and slip from it, we blame it on genetics. The first time it gets a little tough, many of us are quick to see the path as a dead end. But here is what you must believe: you do not always have to think negative. If you cannot get in, go up. If you cannot get through on this level, go up to a higher level. Sometimes the reason it seems like you are restricted or there is a block somewhere is because you are at the wrong level, and sometimes disappointments will teach you to climb up to the next one.

The best way to deal with disappointment is to learn how to see it as a way to keep moving forward. Don't let the roadblocks stop your forward momentum; accept that you've stumbled, and then figure out how to keep moving. You can only pull through disappointments if you let them go.

Joanie Quinn once talked about "The Value of Disappointment" in a TEDx Talk. She said, "I'm a mom. I'm a mediocre mom. And […] by disappointing my children over the years, they ended up building a muscle that I didn't even know they needed. By having a mediocre mom, my kids ended up learning the most valuable lesson of all time: how to handle disappointment."

Now, don't misunderstand me; it's not a great thing to

describe yourself as "a mediocre mom." But the crux of her explanation is that you must create a balance between making your children comfortable and forcing them to grow. As Quinn notes, most parents these days focus too much of their energy on trying to keep their kids happy. But guess what: kids can still end up disappointed as they become overindulged. So, rather than pamper kids till they are spoiled, you should try to train them to deal with disappointments in life.

Life isn't perfect, and while family should always aim to be a source of happiness and peace, it's a disservice to our youth to make them think their lives will always be easy. I received similar lessons early in life, and it made me understand that I would not always get what I wanted. If you cannot deal with disappointments, you cannot handle success. Successful people thrive not only when all is well, but also when times are hard.

Trying times may come, but if you are going to be led through the fire, you must believe there is a way out. Reading through Moses' conversations with God in the Bible (especially at the time he is leading the children of Israel out of Egypt), I find myself wondering what would have happened if he'd decided to throw in the towel—if he'd chosen to give up and bring the people back to Egypt, as they'd requested. Thank goodness he never quit—they could have missed out on everything God had in store for them.

You must love success, because that passion is going to allow you to get up and keep trying when disappointment comes. As a matter of fact, when you love success and you start going for it, something happens. And guess what it is? Failure.

Yes, you are going to fail ten times or a hundred times, or maybe even a thousand times, but that is okay. Failure is not permanent; neither is a disappointment. You'll get right back up and keep going, and this time, you are going to be stronger, wiser, and more driven than you have ever been. And for every ten disappointments, you will land one success. In the spirit of something Sylvester Stallone once said: You must love success so much that you are willing to fail ten times before you can succeed once.

Seizing Opportunities

Opportunity is a subtle phenomenon, often misrepresented as an obvious treasure when in actuality it is the map, the road, and the courage to move forward. Opportunity is not the moon, the sun, or the stars; it is the staircase that takes you higher, the pieces that come together to form your universe. And when the light comes on and your eyes open, when you wake up and breathe your first breath, understand that you are breathing in opportunity. It is not what you look at; it is what you see. And befitting of the message, it is easy to push this away as insignificance or fluff. But let me ask you this: how does one person turn adversity into the very reason they succeed, and another turn that same adversity into a ball and chain? Why do some run towards chaos and others retreat? How can one person transform a loss into a win, while another person views that same defeat as the end? Well, the answer is quite simple: did you seek out the opportunity, or did you not? That is the question. And when you strip life down of its complexities, the patterns become apparent.

The people who win never ask if their goals are even possible. They never turn back simply because the door is shut. No; they begin with the premise that it can be done. They believe there must be an open door somewhere when one door closes.

So, you may be asking, how? How can I make this a reality? How can I turn the world around me, how can I position the events taking place—whether challenging, strenuous, reassuring, or anything in between—to lift me up? What exactly is the opportunity? Without that realization, you will never have your pot of gold. It begins in your head and is projected out. They say, "Fake it till you make it." Well, I will tell you there is something to that. Because if you never put a dream, or a goal, or a plan into existence, no matter how small, it simply fails to exist. You must see your city on the hill when it is still just rocks. It is not a waste, it is not stupid, and it is not irrational, because you know what it can be. Doubters do not see, but you do. And that is an opportunity. Their wasteland is your future empire. Their free time is your launch pad. Their hopelessness is your reassurance. Their rejection is your acceptance. They see blank space, but you see infinity waiting to be unpacked and expanded. Throw away the "ifs" and start asking how.

Opportunities are everywhere, but remember, they are not the sun, the moon, or the stars. They do not always shine bright for all to see. Seize every opportunity that comes your way, and where there are none, create one!

Chapter Ten
MENTORS

Son, do what your father tells you and never forget what your mother taught you. Keep their words with you always, locked in your heart. Their teaching will lead you when you travel, protect you at night, and advise you during the day. Their instructions are a shining light; their correction can teach you how to live.
—Book of Proverbs

Mentorship is something we hardly talk about these days. People prefer to go their way, do their thing, and figure things will work out on their own without submitting to anyone or going to anyone for guidance. But it does not often work like that. From my experience, getting a mentor is key to attaining success in life.

Contrary to what most people believe to be true, mentorship is not a one-way street. It is not about one person advising the other. Both people are showing up to give and learn. Just like in friendship, you need to cultivate a relationship and relate well with each other.

But first, before you go all out looking for a mentor, you need to believe in yourself. No one will believe in you if you do not believe in you, and no one likes to be a mentor to someone who has yet to get things figured out for themselves. A mentor is not supposed to build your life for you; they are only there to guide you on how to build your life.

One important thing to note is that role models are not mentors. They are completely different. As a university undergraduate, I had people I loved to read about; stories of men like Thomas Edison and Walt Disney inspired me a lot. Each time I read about them, I found something to spur me to take a new, bold step towards success. Now, those were my role models, not my mentors. A role model is someone you love to imitate, someone who you aspire to be like. But mentors are trusted persons with wisdom to offer. They guide you personally and take responsibility for your growth and progress on all sides. Your mentor knows you deeply, and uses this bond to motivate and push you, whereas you are a total stranger to a role model.

(To be fair, role models could, very rarely, become mentors if you happened to have the chance to meet and deeply connect with them; but this would require overcoming the hurdle of idealization).

Finding a Mentor

You do not just wake up one sunny morning, walk up to a stranger, and request mentoring. You must have first had some relationship with such a person that has developed over time and observed facets of their life or methods that you desire.

The book of Proverbs says, *"The way of a fool is right in his own eyes, but a wise man listens to advice"* (Proverbs 12:15). The message is quite clear: anyone who is going to make it big in his field or reach the peak of his potential in life must be willing to hearken unto counsel.

To gain a trusted adviser, you must be worth advising. Your prospective mentors must be able to see something in you that is worth their time to nurture, so that when you flourish, you will be able to offer something to them as well. This is not to say that no mentor can act altruistically, but those with years of experience want to find a trustworthy, able candidate as a mentee so they know that their wisdom is not being squandered. Your suggestions, opinions, and ideas are potential resources of unprecedented value.

The first and most important step when it comes to finding a mentor is knowing yourself. Mentoring is a relationship, and so understanding your own strengths and weaknesses is key for your development. Of course, you may not be able to decipher every key trait or lacking quality yet, and your mentor will be able to help address this, but you shouldn't expect your mentor to identify and solve all your problems for you. You need to be able to show that you have put work into yourself—work that can be multiplied and applied to different avenues.

Before approaching any person for mentorship, you should reflect on your network and know what kind of person you desire to be your mentor. If you've recently survived a family gathering and there were kids present, you definitely heard this question: *So, what do you want to be when you grow up?* I think it is a fair question to ask of ourselves our entire lives. And implied by this question is not only what you want to be, but who you want to be like.

In every profession there are heroes, rock stars, and trendsetters. And in whatever field you find yourself, there are persons you'll admire and desire to match up to. It might be someone you can learn from simply by watching them, reading what they write, or maybe even listening to a TED Talk about them. Reaching out and connecting with someone whom you respect could result in a mentorship. You can research them on LinkedIn and other social media platforms. Study their backgrounds, what made them who they are today. See if you share any acquaintances through friends, family, or university that would be willing to set up a warm, friendly connection. And if you keep going with that, chances are that you will put them in a better position to say "Yes" to your mentorship request.

As important as self-discovery, warm connections, and all these things are, they cannot work without courage. Sometimes it is quite difficult to walk up to someone we admire; the idea of rejection is heart-wrenching. But you cannot let fear of the uncertain future hold you back from potential rewards.

Types of Mentors

I have always been incredibly lucky to have mentors around me. And from my still-developing experience in mentoring and mentorship, I have come to realize that there are three different types of mentors you can find for yourself in life—a sponsor, a guide, or a coach.

A sponsor is someone who puts their reputation on the line for you. They are willing to put their name behind yours to get you access to people, jobs, or opportunities that you would not have if they didn't support you. Sponsors do not like to give any guidance themselves, and this is what makes them unique. They instead have ties to those who are in a better place to offer assistance, and thus connect you.

The second type of mentor is the guide. These people tend to be about fifteen to twenty years ahead on the very path you wish to tread. Guides understand the process because of their direct experience, and they are aware of what it means to grow. They can relate to every stage, and so they know just how to take you from where you currently are to where you wish to be. They are the ones who ask about your next step and give you the chance to trust your own decisions.

And then, there is the coach mentor—paid or not. They have probably not fully walked the path and may not have a sizeable enough reputation to sponsor you. But they make insightful remarks and ask scrutinizing questions to make you examine where you want to go, as well as what is working and what is not working. And they listen deeply to your answers, paying attention to every detail and taking note of every word you utter so they can track your progress.

There is really no rule that states what kind of mentor you ought to have and at what point. If you have access to all, then go ahead. Having more than one type of mentor will only broaden your horizons.

Of these three mentor types, there are five different styles of teaching:

- companion
- planter of seeds
- catalyst
- demonstrator
- mirror

A companion is someone who positively supports you as you progress, while a planter of seeds is one who sees in you possibilities, opportunities, and other qualities you have yet to see in yourself. A catalyst pushes you and puts you into contact with opportunities and challenges that force you to become a better version of yourself. The demonstrator is someone who can talk about how they have overcome similar challenges. Lastly, the mirror is one who repeats what they hear from you. This sounds a bit odd but is, in fact, quite powerful. Nothing feels more refreshing than hearing someone speak back to you what you have just shared about your dreams and goals in life. It shows that they care about who you are and what you wish to be, and will help you recognize any potential flaws in your plans.

Mentorship can come in any shape and form. It would be foolhardy to think mentors can only be gray-haired elders who've long since retired. Many of the great mentors in my life have been coach types who repeated back my actions, or sponsoring companions who inspired me with simple words that snowballed into great ideas.

One common reason people choose a poor mentor is that they only seek the well-known people—those who are high up there with every kind of success you can think of in life. And while that is not explicitly harmful, it might not always be the right choice. You may not need someone whose level of success is miles above your own; what you need is someone who can discern your abilities and open your eyes to your hidden potentials, someone who can listen to you speak for hours and gauge where you're at and how far you have left to go.

Mentee Etiquette

While you won't find a set-in-stone code of conduct for mentorship, there are certain things to steer clear of as you're being mentored. The very first thing to avoid as a mentee is gossip. I used to have a mentee who would come to my office for our monthly meetings and ask, "Is everyone getting along at the company? Did you hear about what that manager said?" For goodness' sake, I was not just going to share all the drama I had heard to this person. He was looking for gossip, and that turned me off completely.

I had another mentee who worked with me for over five months, and each time we got together, I would ask, "Did my advice help you in any way?" To my disappointment, she'd reply with various forms of, "Oh, you know, I have been too busy," or "I didn't think it was going to work, so I didn't even try it out." But then, she'd try to get more advice from me. It was an exasperating scenario, to say the least.

Learn to always take your mentor seriously. You should value their time, effort, and everything they give. If, in any case, you are not able to implement whatever advice you are given, you could inform your mentor about it as the situation occurs. It does not hurt; it only makes you more responsible and accountable, and your mentor may be able to provide alternative advice.

What is most important is that you remember that mentorship is a relationship between two people, which will continue to grow and adapt with you both. As a mentee, you shouldn't feel restricted or dictated; mentoring ought to be enjoyed and not endured. It becomes something to endure when you are not feeling the flow any longer. Revel in the relationship and make every single moment with your mentor count.

Be Humble

Humility is key in mentoring, and it cannot be faked. It is easy to stay low and mild-mannered when you need to get something from somebody. I mean, everyone does this, even kids—one minute they are meek and lowly, the next, when they have gotten what they needed, they are boastful with victory. You need to remind yourself to keep your feet firmly on the ground after experiencing your first doses of success.

After you have gained a certain level of knowledge, the temptation to stretch your wings might set in: you no longer see a need to visit your mentor, and you begin to doubt their advice. But here is my counsel: be humble. No matter how high you have gone—or how high you think you have gone—you can still learn from your mentor.

If you are ever going to land your dream job, attain your desired height, or occupy your longed-for space, you must be willing to remain committed to learning. Isaac Newton once said, "If I have seen further, it is by standing on the shoulders of giants." He understood something we all need to be reminded of: we are at our best when we rely upon the wisdom and knowledge of those who have come before us.

Successful Mentoring

Mentoring is, at its core, training or disciplining others. Of course, anyone can be a mentor. You do not need to be perfect to become an effective mentor; you only need to have the ability and willingness to impart what you have gained unto others.

As a mentor, you teach both skills and character. While skills are usually taught intentionally, character is more often taught unintentionally. The simple fact that you spend so much time together means your mentee will, subconsciously, pick up your manner of speaking, reactions, and ways of approach. A good mentee will watch you like a hawk to emulate your abilities.

You should only mentor a person who is ready, willing, and able to grow. Everyone loves growth, but not everyone can endure its process. A mentee must be one who is faithful, available, and teachable.

Effective mentoring requires a customized growth plan that fits the individual, and both the mentor and mentee should be on a personal growth program. When you are mentoring and you want to teach a specific task, there is a four-step process that you should follow:

1) *I do the task, while you watch and learn.*

2) *We do the task together.*

3) *You do the task, and I watch and offer feedback.*

And finally,

4) *You do the task.*

This way, you can ensure your mentoring has been completely effective.

To be a good mentor, you have got to expect results. The key to exponential growth is to make sure that you do not just mentor anyone; if you want to grow exponentially, make sure to mentor someone who will, in turn, mentor others. If you want to be successful, you must be teachable and a lifelong learner.

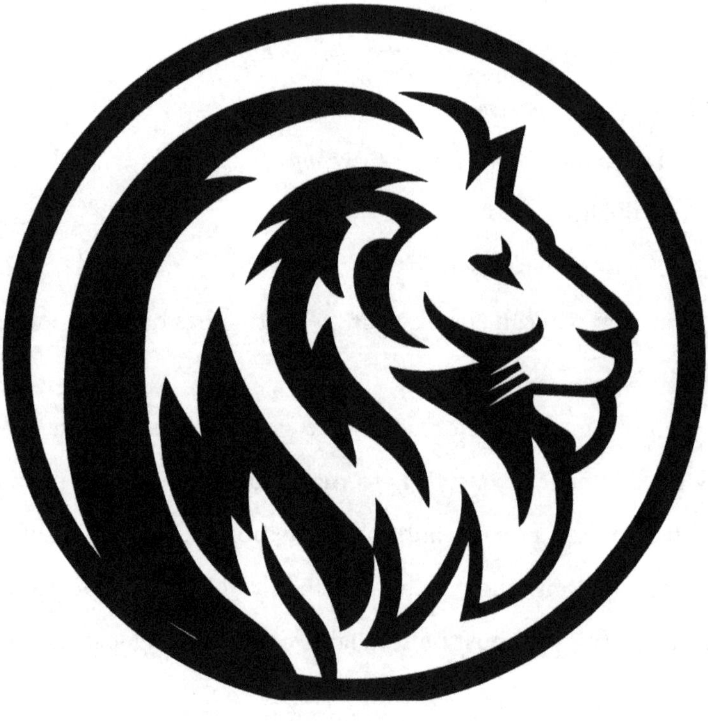

Chapter Eleven
FAITH

Now faith is confidence in what we hope for and assurance about what we do not see.
—Book of Hebrews

The urge to quit is very real. Truth be told, every champion has felt it. Every soldier has felt it. Every president has felt it. Every king has felt it. We can all feel like the race is not worth running when the odds get stacked against us, and things begin to fall apart. And at one point or the other, we have all had the urge to give up on our goals of success. In His days, Jesus Christ did all that was required of Him and all that He came to the world to do. But at the climax of His journey, He felt like bypassing the whole thing and starting all over. Recall Jesus prayed to God in the garden at Gethsemane, saying, *"My Father, if it is possible, may this cup be taken from me"* (Matthew 26:39). He was drained of strength at that point and was unable to drink from the cup that was set before Him.

It happens to all of us, in one form or another.

The journey to success gets tougher and tougher as we move on. As a result, we are prone to almost losing faith like Jesus almost did—of course, Jesus stayed resolute through His tribulations, and that's why He is the ultimate role model. He went back to His Father, and this time, it was for submission to His will.

Faith is not just believing in some seemingly impossible stuff. You know, many of us grew up with some erroneous beliefs about faith that nearly cost us good fortune; we think of faith as a passive thing or something extremely supernatural. But faith is so much more! It is a substance, an active movement, and something quite practical.

Faith is a conscious and deliberate progression towards your dreams when the odds are against you. Do not get me wrong; Faith is believing God. Faith is trusting in the divine. Faith is being positive about life. But the most profound explanation of faith for me is what James writes in the second chapter of his Epistle:

> My friends, what good is it for one of you to say that you have faith if your actions do not prove it? Can

that faith save you? Suppose there are brothers or sisters who need clothes and don't have enough to eat. What good is there in your saying to them, 'God bless you! Keep warm and eat well!'—if you don't give them the necessities of life? So it is with faith: if it is alone and includes no actions, then it is dead. (James 2:14-17)

Faith works only when it is done the right way.

Trust in God

You have heard these words since you were in Sunday school. But you will discover as time passes how difficult they are to obey.

Of course, I have no way of knowing what the future holds for you. All losses are painful, and you will be brought back repeatedly to the words in Proverbs 3:5-6 of the Bible: *"Always trust the [Lord] completely. Do not think that your wisdom is enough. Remember the [Lord] in everything that you do. If you do, [H]e will show you the right way to go."*

Faith in God requires absolute trust; that is where the transforming power lies. Faith moves the unseen into the realm of the seen and brings all that is yet a dream into reality. But now, we find it difficult to trust God and believe that our goals are achievable. There are several reasons for this.

First off, we are to blame for our perceived independence and reliance on false idols. God designed us with self-determinism, but sometimes, as we go through life solving problems and getting ourselves out of tough situations, we become too prideful. We begin to think we don't need anyone else, that we are self-sufficient. And then something terrible happens, and we are brought back down to humility.

Our other folly is misunderstanding blessings during times of hardship. We should nurture our friendships and connections with loved ones, and be pleased with our successes financially and personally, but when we begin to value these over God, they become detrimental. You cannot put all of your dependence on mere Earthly subjects. They will become crutches and distractions.

God is not a distant master who observes but does not interfere. God's chief concern is with His creation, as is evidenced throughout the Bible. God is closer and more accessible than most of us are willing to admit, because accepting how near and present He is can be overwhelming. But take comfort; God desires for us to become great even more so than we desire it for ourselves. But the problem is that we do not believe it.

Humans have cultivated the habit of worry. And that is another major hindrance to achieving success in life. Many of us are much better at worrying than we are at trusting; if we were to put together a worry list, it would outrun our prayer list. You are worried right now about something—let us say it is something related to your schoolwork, or maybe your finances. Here are my words of encouragement: you will never have enough money; you will never have enough of anything. You can only decide enough is enough by being content. Worry solves no problem, and it makes nothing better. Rather than worrying over your next step, your closed doors, or your next opportunity, trust that all will be well and believe you will come out on top.

I have a longtime friend who was raised with four brothers in Southwest Texas. They grew up on a ranch where they eked out a living. My friend wound up getting into Baylor, going on to UCLA Law School, and earning his degree in law, and has since become an exceptionally fine attorney in the Southern California area. One of his brothers stayed back at the ranch to cultivate and develop it, while the others moved away, including my friend. And the one who stayed, along with his wife, turned the ranch into something more successful. He grew crops, bred cattle, sold them both little by little, and finally became financially stable.

Then the Texas wildfires of 2011 swept through their area, and the couple knew they would probably lose all the cattle. So they simply opened the gate and, amazingly, those animals instinctively knew where to go to find shelter and safety, and so they fled. The man and his wife threw all they could into their pickup and drove away. They returned several days later when it was safe.

Everything was scourged and melted, including the metal roof on the barn—it had buckled and warped. And my friend told me what his brother said then: "We realized at that moment that our faith would either kick into action, or we would move far away from the God we had loved and served." They chose the former. They determined they would rebuild, and they are in the process right now.

Faith sees the odds and acknowledges them, but moves deliberately past them. It picks up the broken pieces and rises to build again. Whatever your challenges, trusting God will help you to acknowledge that He is all-knowing and all-powerful. And when you diligently obey His pattern for life, He will also fulfill His promise to help and bless you till you attain glory. We are all human, and we all have limitations. God is the only one who can create something out of nothing. So, learn to trust Him.

Faith Can Be Taught; Faith Can Be Learned

Once, while I was speaking to some folks on the power of faith and how faith can change everything, someone asked, "Do you think it is possible to learn faith?"

And even though I was not sure what to say next, I found myself replying, "Yes, faith can be learned. It is possible to learn faith." Here is my thought: faith is a substance, as the Bible puts it (Hebrews 11:1). And this means it is something quite tangible. Religion can be taught in an academic sense at Christian schools, but how can one learn faith—to believe?

First off, I would like us to consider faith a habit—it is not just an action or something you do once in a blue moon to feel okay. It is a habit. Faith will become part of your core makeup, evident in the way you talk, the way you react, and your perception of life.

Just as you cannot brew hot and cold simultaneously, you cannot think both positively and negatively. Anyone who wishes to build great faith in life and develop a right disposition towards success must deliberately fill up their mind with good thoughts. Spending more time around people with deep faithlessness does no good to your faith. People who talk negatively and see more reasons why a thing should fail than why it should succeed are toxic to your faith. It is just a matter of time before you begin to think like them and reason along with them. Their actions, reactions, and inactions are teachings in themselves. You may not realize it, but they are slowly culturing your mind to be like theirs.

Commit your time to those with aggressive faith—those who will cheer you on when you feel burned out, those who will inspire you to live when life ceases to make sense, and those who will remind you of your dreams and aspirations. Now, you don't have to exclude those without strong faith, nor do you have to split hairs about their exact theologies, but individuals with strong beliefs that you agree with will help you tackle doubts. With them by your side, you will find it easier to move towards better days.

The logic is simple. Suppose everyone in my circle complains about how things are constantly going bad, how progress gradually seems impossible, and how success is a myth. In that case, I would have no cause to speak otherwise. Even if I did, my group would most likely have their way of influencing my thoughts. So, the first rule of the faith game is: flock with people of like minds. Besides, you must speak positive things to yourself. *"I believed; therefore I have spoken"* —that's what the Bible says in 2 Corinthians 4:13.

Our minds are made to process and accept concepts almost continuously. One of the easiest ways to delete negative thoughts is to speak positive things. When you find yourself doubting all that you once believed, thinking thoughts like, *"Am I even sure this will work out?," "What if this does not end the way I envisaged?,"* and *"Who is going to help if this fails again?"* rise and make professions to the contrary.

Professions have a way of reassuring the mind of all that

will be even though it has not come to be yet. They erase every conflicting thought and align your thoughts with your words. In Joshua 1:6-8, God said to Joshua:

> Be strong and do not be afraid. You will lead these people to take the land. That is the land that I promised to give to their *ancestors*. Be strong and do not be afraid. Be very careful to do all the things that Moses *commanded* you do to. Then everything will go well with you, everywhere that you go. You must keep on speaking about the words of God's *law*. Think about what it says, all the time. Be careful to obey it. Then you will do well, and you will win.

This passage establishes a connection between speaking and doing. When you discuss the same topics repeatedly, they register in your subconscious, and in no time, you begin to act accordingly. The law of sowing and reaping applies here; if you sow negative words, you will reap negative results. Do not join the clique of those who speak evil or derive pleasure from talking of impossibilities; you will not grow in faith that way. Talk positive. Talk well.

Another great way to learn faith is to read texts that bolster your conviction. Over the years, I have built so much confidence from reading from men who have exercised great faith in their life's journeys—the likes of William Branham, Jesse Duplantis, Benny Hinn, and many others. They inspire me and give me a reason to keep pushing.

Of all the faith books you would find on bookstores' shelves these days, the Bible is the best. I consider it the best because it contains practical experiences of men who went through thick and thin to get their dreamland, and it shows just how you can navigate through life by faith in God. Let us look at this passage from Hebrews 11:1-3:

> This is what it means to *trust* God: We will be sure about the things that we hope for. We will be sure in our minds about things that we cannot even see. It was because of their *faith* that God said good things about the people of long ago. Because of faith, we understand how God made the *universe*. He spoke [H]is [W]ord to make it happen. In that way, God made all the things that we can see. He made them from things nobody could see.

Hebrews also tells the tales of different outstanding Biblical characters: Abel, Enoch, Noah, Abraham, Moses, and a host of others. The people didn't see God, but they held His word as truth and obeyed Him to the very last. You can hardly finish those faith stories without feeling a need to push further.

And yeah, prayer works. You should pray, too. When you pray, you are trading your weaknesses, doubts, and limitations for God's strength. You are yielding to a power that is far above yours. Prayer makes faith possible. You pray to God, and He strengthens your convictions.

Just as you learn to build faith by doing one or all of the things I have mentioned above, you can teach faith, too. Make yourself that one person who imparts strength rather than one who saps it. Do not talk about things that would make other persons lose faith. The Bible says it all: *"When you speak to people, always speak kind words. Say things that will help them. Then, when someone asks you a question, you will know how to reply"* (Colossians 4:6).

The words we speak can make or mar. So, be mindful of what you say and how you say what you say. It is far better to keep mum and listen to what others have to say than say something that would cause others to lose faith.

Words Are Powerful

Just about everybody you encounter is going through something you'd never pick up on from their appearance. Even the fiercest internal battles are hidden from the outside world. I hope that you will embrace the potential of what God might do through a single word of encouragement. You have no idea how God could use you to offer someone hope and build someone's faith.

There is so much negativity in the world today. All over the news are experiences and events that make you want to give up on life itself. The social media space is not any better; you can't scroll through your feed without feeling depressed or discouraged. Conversations about current events are dominated with heartbreaking facts and overwhelming grief. And a lot of people in this polarized world can be so incredibly critical and so undeniably hateful. But guess what—there is hope.

There is hope when we cease to talk about the things that break us down emotionally or tear us apart physically, and instead focus on the things that make for success. It is high time we stepped in to lift others up with our words. It is high time we brought words of hope, words of encouragement, and words of assurance to everyone who is on the verge of giving up.

The words we speak are filled with power. Our words can build up, and our words can pull down. The tongue has the power of life and death, and it has the power of success and failure (Proverbs 18:21). Whatever you do, speak words that build your faith and that of those around you, and not the other way 'round.

Do Not Doubt Yourself

Proverbs 22:8 says, *"He who sows iniquity will reap sorrow, [a]nd the rod of his anger will fail."* When you refuse to allow any doubt into your mind, no doubt from others will ever cloud your judgment. When you create a strong mind for yourself, no others will defeat you with their words or judgments. The only person that controls what you believe in is you. You are your number one fan.

Others have no say in who you will become; you do. You decide what you want to make out of life; you decide where you want to be in life; you decide how to get your desired end. Whether or not you achieve your life purpose is solely your business. No matter how involved others are in the affairs of your life, the truth remains that your life is yours, and yours alone. You either allow the opinions others have to become a reality in your life, or you create your fate.

The greatest challenges and obstacles any human will face are their doubts, fears, and conditioned thoughts.

If you want to live your dream, you will have to fight for it. You will have to fight the greatest battles of your life. You will have to battle the external enemy—people who do not believe you, people who do you wrong, and people who put you down. You will have to battle the intimate enemy—those close to you who might do you wrong, those who maybe do not believe in you, or those who want the best for you but their idea of support is to remind you of what cannot be done or what should not be attempted.

But worst of all is the internal enemy.

You will have to battle what seems like an army in your head—an army of doubt, fear of failure, fear of judgment, and lack of belief. The voices inside your head will say, *"I am not good enough. I am not worthy. I want to do this, but I can't."* No greater pain can be inflicted on you than by your internal enemy. Your own thoughts will cause you more pain than anyone or anything. They can be likened to a terrorist living in your soul.

When you learn to control and direct your mind, you can direct that internal voice so that it works for you rather than against you. You can learn to have it work for you by creating a compelling future—a future you will be proud to achieve, a future where you can look proudly behind you and give thanks to God. It is not just enough to have goals; you must have meaningful goals and keep your eyes fixed on achieving them.

Faith Is Intentional

One reliable way to silence your negative voices is to understand what your purpose in life really is. What are you doing it all for? Why are you pushing this hard? When you know these things, you can forge gallantly ahead and make all your dreams come true.

In Proverbs 3:6, King Solomon said, "*In all thy ways acknowledge [H]im, and [H]e shall direct thy paths.*" It is not easy to give yourself up to God, to relinquish the mortal hold you have over your life and accept that the overarching plan of the Almighty is one that you fit into. But it is essential.

Faith is intentional, and it takes one who is deliberate about hitting the mark to grow it. You need to be committed to the course. You need to stay true to a daily practice of faith. You need to put all else aside and walk consciously on the path of success. Cut out your mindless habits and replace them with daily work on your character. The voice in your head will only work for you if you work for it. Fill up your mind with strength and optimism, and you will live a life full of strength and optimism.

Growing in Faith

There is a reason many people start out on the journey of faith today with so much zeal and passion but break down to disbelief as time goes on. Often, we fail to acknowledge the fact that we are on an actual journey, and yesterday's strength might not suffice for today's sojourn. The false assumption that we have gathered all the courage there is to muster is why people still fail these days. You need to grow your faith; you need to increase your strength.

In growing faith, every second counts, and every single step matters. The more you take breaks or relax on building your faith, the more you become prone to fear and doubt. You must be willing to grow your faith till it cannot be grown any further.

It is easy to exercise faith when you experience certain minor setbacks. But there are life challenges that will throw you completely off balance if you are not well guarded.

You and I were born with the gift to make the world a better place. God gave every man the ability to transform the world around them. And even if we did not improve things massively, we could still make changes right now; we could encourage and compliment people. We could solve problems. We could pick up trash, fix things, and offer new ideas. As you grow, you become a bigger source for the rest of life to express itself through you.

You were put here for a reason, and God Himself best knows that reason. So, figure out your purpose in life, understand it, and seek to walk intentionally towards its fulfillment. Every process of growth takes time. It is impossible to become a faith monster by reading a few books or listening to a couple of sermons. You must cultivate a faith lifestyle and live your entire life practicing faith.

CLOSING REMARKS

I hope you have found value in these words. Now the question is: what are you going to do with the wealth of knowledge you have gained not only from this book, but throughout your life? There is a folktale about a rich king who called all his war generals together and told them about the secret to his wealth. All of the generals marveled and expressed their admiration at the greatness of the king. However, one of them put the information to work and became just as rich as the king. Life is shaped more by what you do than by what you know. And when you put all you know into action, there's no telling the heights you'll achieve. So, are you merely going to remain still while you possess knowledge that can change your life, or will you take steps to make your world better today?

To bring these lessons full circle, remember that nothing stands tall without a strong foundation. You need to start somewhere, and I implore you to take responsibility. One quite common myth you will find in American culture these days is that we all hold a right to be great. Some extremists believe that life owes us all the best things and must never deprive us of them. But that is false. Thoughts like this should be grappled, battered, and kicked to the curb—they are way too elusive to be true. Rather than build your life around such tales, you should get this bitter truth into your head and allow it sink deep: you are responsible for your own life. Your failures, your options, and your happiness—they are all your responsibilities. This is the foundation, the beginning, and the first step to becoming successful.

References

1. Brown, Brené. *Gifts of Imperfection*. Random House Publishing Group, 2020.

2. Canfield, Jack. *The Success Principles*, 2007.

3. Dweck, Carol. *Mindset: The New Psychology of Success.* Random House, 2006.

4. Collins, Jim. *Good to Great: Why Some Companies Make the Leap . . . and Others Don't.* New York: HarperCollins, 2001.

5. Collins, Marva, and Civia Tamarkin. *Marva Collins' Way: Returning to Excellence in Education.* Los Angeles: Jeremy Tarcher, 1982/1990.

6. Csikszentmihalyi, Mihaly. *Flow: The Psychology of Optimal Experience.* New York: Harper & Row, 1990.

7. Davis, Stan. *Schools Where Everyone Belongs: Practical Strategies*

for Reducing

8. *Bullying*. Wayne, ME: Stop Bullying Now, 2003.

9. Edwards, Betty. *The New Drawing on the Right Side of the Brain*. New York: Tarcher/Putnam, 1979/1999.

10. Mahmood SS, Levy D, Vasan RS, Wang TJ. The Framingham Heart Study and the epidemiology of cardiovascular disease: a historical perspective. *Lancet*. (2014).

11. Collazo, Raphael. "The Power of Association - Who Do You Associate with?" Medium. Medium, November 8, 2018. https://medium.com/@recollaz/the-power-of-association-who-do-you-associate-with-af108c824111.

12. Young, Emma. "Lifting the Lid on the Unconscious." New Scientist, July 25, 2018. https://www.newscientist.com/article/mg23931880-400-lifting-the-lid-on-the-unconscious.

13. Baer, Drake. "Malcolm Gladwell Explains What Everyone Gets Wrong about His Famous '10,000 Hour Rule'." Business Insider. Business Insider, June 2, 2014. https://www.businessinsider.com/malcolm-gladwell-explains-the-10000-hour-rule-2014-6.

14. Diane, Jasmine. "Your Dreams Are Valid." Jasmine Diane. Jasmine Diane, July 18, 2018. https://www.jasminediane.

com/blog/your-dreams-are-valid.

15. Nicklaus, Jack, and Ken Bowden. *Golf My Way*. London: Heinemann, 1976.

16. Cohn, Patrick. "Sports Visualization for Athletes: Sports Psychology Articles." Sports Psychology Articles | Sport Psychology Articles for Athletes, Coaches, and Sports Parents, October 13, 2020. https://www.peaksports.com/sports-psychology-blog/sports-visualization-athletes/.

17. Usó-Doménech, J.L., Nescolarde-Selva, J. *What are Belief Systems?* (2016). https://doi.org/10.1007/s10699-015-9409-z

18. Godin, Seth. "The Difference between a Failure and a Mistake." Seth's Blog, December 18, 2011. https://seths.blog/2011/12/the-difference-between-a-failure-and-a-mistake/.

19. Pink, Daniel H. *When: The Scientific Secrets of Perfect Timing*. Edinburgh: Canongate, 2019.

20. Yoonsuck Choe, Jaerock Kwon, and Ji Ryang Chung. *Time, Consciousness, and Mind Uploading*. International Journal of Machine Consciousness. 2012.

21. Lachman, Walen. *Social support and Strain from Partner, Family,*

and Friends: Costs and Benefits for Men and Women in Adulthood. 2000

22. Stone AA, Schwartz JE, Schkade D, Schwarz N, Krueger A, Kahneman D. A population approach to the study of emotion: diurnal rhythms of a working day examined with the Day Reconstruction Method. Emotion. 2006

23. Bible Versions — Contemporary English Version (CEV), King James Version (KJV), Good News Translation (GNT), New International Version (NIV), English Standard Version (ESV), EasyEnglish Bible (EASY), and New King James Version (NKJV)

24. https://ieltsliz.com/determination-my-story/;https://www.youtube.com/channel/UCKPpfQUSfHhesyjbskDKSEg (IELTS Liz)

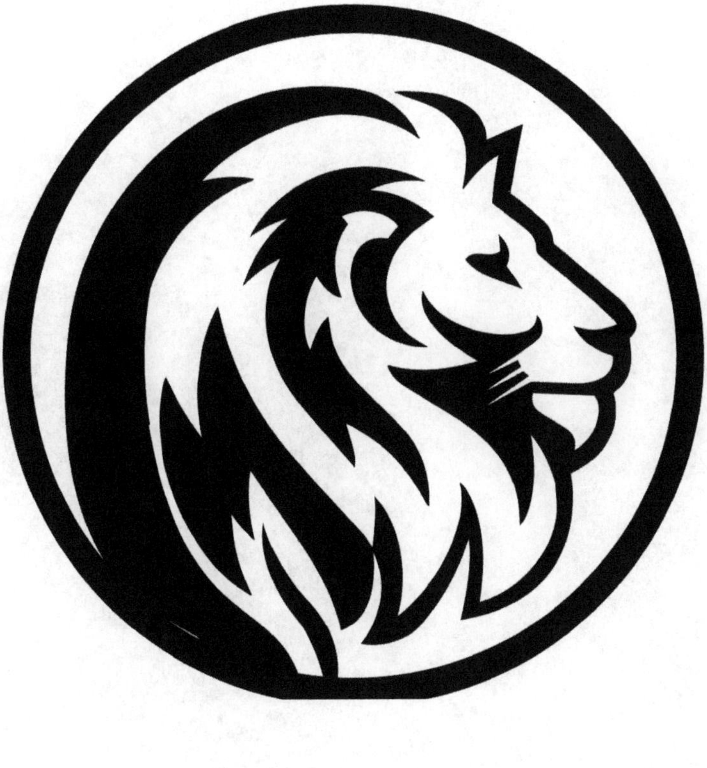

CPSIA information can be obtained
at www.ICGtesting.com
Printed in the USA
BVHW090128311021
620331BV00004B/21/J

9 781942 549956